بسم الله الرحمن الرحيم

ABOUT THE AUTHOR

Under the pen-name HARUN YAHYA, the author has published many books on political and faith-related issues. An important body of his work deals with the materialistic world view and the impact of it in world history and politics. (The pen-name is formed from the names 'Harun' [Aaron] and 'Yahya' [John] in the esteemed memory of the two Prophets who struggled against infidelity.)

His works include The 'Secret Hand' in Bosnia, The Holocaust Hoax, Behind the Scenes of Terrorism, Israel's Kurdish Card, A National Strategy for Turkey, Solution: The Morals of the Qur'an, Darwin's Antagonism Against the Turks, The Calamities Darwinism Caused Humanity, The Evolution Deceit, Perished Nations, The Golden Age, Allah's Artistry in Colour, Glory is Everywhere, The Truth of the Life of This World, Confessions of Evolutionists, The Blunders of Evolutionists, The Dark Magic of Darwinism, The Religion of Darwinism, The Qur'an Leads the Way to Science, The Real Origin of Life, The Creation of the Universe, Miracles of the Qur'an, The Design in Nature, Self-Sacrifice and Intelligent Behaviour Models in Animals, Eternity Has Already Begun, Children Darwin Was Lying!, The End of Darwinism, Deep Thinking, Timelessness and the Reality of Fate, Never Plead Ignorance, The Secrets of DNA, The Miracle of the Atom, The Miracle in the Cell, The Miracle of the Immune System, The Miracle in the Eye, The Creation Miracle in Plants, The Miracle in the Spider, The Miracle in the Ant, The Miracle in the Gnat, The Miracle in the Honeybee, The Miracle of Seed, The Miracle in the Termite.

Among his booklets are The Mystery of the Atom, The Collapse of the Theory of Evolution: The Fact of Creation, The Collapse of Materialism, The End of Materialism, The Blunders of Evolutionists 1, The Blunders of Evolutionists 2, The Microbiological Collapse of Evolution, The Fact of Creation, The Collapse of the Theory of Evolution in 20 Questions, The Biggest Deception in the History of Biology: Darwinism.

The author's other works on Quranic topics include: Ever Thought About the Truth?, Devoted to Allah, Abandoning the Society of Ignorance, Paradise, The Theory of Evolution, The Moral Values of the Qur'an, Knowledge of the Qur'an, Qur'an Index, Emigrating for the Cause of Allah, The Character of Hypocrites in the Qur'an, The Secrets of the Hypocrite, The Names of Allah, Communicating the Message and Disputing in the Qur'an, The Basic Concepts in the Qur'an, Answers from the Qur'an, Death Resurrection Hell, The Struggle of the Messengers, The Avowed Enemy of Man: Satan, Idolatry, The Religion of the Ignorant, The Arrogance of Satan, Prayer in the Qur'an, The Importance of Conscience in the Qur'an, The Day of Resurrection, Never Forget, Disregarded Judgements of the Qur'an, Human Characters in the Society of Ignorance, The Importance of Patience in the Qur'an, General Information from the Qur'an, Quick Grasp of Faith 1-2-3, The Crude Reasoning of Disbelief, The Mature Faith, Before You Regret, Our Messengers Say, The Mercy of Believers, The Fear of Allah, The Nightmare of Disbelief, Prophet Isa Will Come, Beauties Presented by the Qur'an for Life, Bouquet of the Beauties of Allah 1-2-3-4, The Iniquity Called "Mockery", The Secret of the Test, The True Wisdom According to the Qur'an, The Struggle with the Religion of Irreligion, The School of Yusuf, The Alliance of the Good, Slanders Spread Against Muslims Throughout History, The Importance of Following the Good Word, Why Do You Deceive Yourself?, Islam: The Religion of Ease, Enthusiasm and Vigor in the Qur'an, Seeing Good in Everything, How does the Unwise Interpret the Qur'an?, Some Secrets of the Qur'an, The Courage of Believers.

NEVER PLEAD IGNORANCE

Published by:
Ta-Ha Publishers Ltd.
1 Wynne Road
London SW9 OBB
United Kingdom

Website: http://www.taha.co.uk
E-Mail: sales @ taha.co.uk

By Harun Yahya
Translated By: Mustapha Ahmad
Edited By: Abdassamad Clarke

A catalog record of this book is available from the British Library
ISBN 1-84200-01-01

Printed and bound by:
Secil Ofset in İstanbul
Address: Yüzyıl Mahallesi MAS-SIT Matbaacılar Sitesi
4. Cadde No:77 Bağcılar- İstanbul / TURKEY

Website: www.harunyahya.org - www.harunyahya.com
www.harunyahya.net

Ta-Ha Publishers Ltd.
1 Wynne Road London SW9 OBB

NEVER PLEAD IGNORANCE

HARUN YAHYA

TO THE READER

In all the books by the author, faith-related issues are explained in the light of the Qur'anic verses and people are invited to learn Allah's words and to live by them. All the subjects that concern Allah's verses are explained in such a way as to leave no room for doubt or question marks in the reader's mind. The sincere, plain and fluent style employed ensures that everyone of every age and from every social group can easily understand the books. This effective and lucid narrative makes it possible to read them in a single sitting. Even those who rigorously reject spirituality are influenced by the facts recounted in these books and cannot refute the truthfulness of their contents.

This book and all the other works of the author can be read individually or discussed in a group at a time of conversation. Those readers who are willing to profit from the books will find discussion very useful in the sense that they will be able to relate their own reflections and experiences to one another.

In addition, it will be a great service to the religion to contribute to the presentation and reading of these books, which are written solely for the good pleasure of Allah. All the books of the author are extremely convincing. For this reason, for those who want to communicate the religion to other people, one of the most effective methods is to encourage them to read these books.

It is hoped that the reader will take time to look through the review of other books on the final pages of the book, and appreciate the rich source of material on faith-related issues, which are very useful and a pleasure to read.

In these books, you will not find, as in some other books, the personal views of the author, explanations based on dubious sources, styles that are unobservant of the respect and reverence due to sacred subjects, nor hopeless, doubt-creating, and pessimistic accounts that create deviations in the heart.

Never Plead Ignorance

Introduction

*E*veryday you wake up to a new day. Getting out of bed, you wash your face, prepare and, most probably, rush somewhere. Like everyone else, you, too, hasten not to be late to school or work and soon find yourself engrossed with everyday routines. In the rapid flow of the day, in school or at work, you struggle to learn something or to meet a deadline, and in the blink of an eye, you notice that it has almost become evening. When you arrive home in the evening, you do your daily housework. Sometimes, just for a change, you visit your friends, go to movies and then return home to sleep. The next morning you start the same vicious circle all over again.

During these daily routines, is it possible that you remain indifferent to other important things in life? In the daily rush of your life, is it possible that you forget, don't notice or **pretend not to grasp** some important things?

The answer of almost everyone should be "Yes." Because the majority of people fail to think or wonder about many details pertaining to their lives. You can start by thinking the following:

While you are in your room reading this book, are you aware that some astonishing incidents are happening? For instance, have you ever thought that you are now moving at 1,670 kilometres an hour through space?

Alternatively, have you ever thought that the room you are in right now occupies a tiny space in the universe, just as if it were a dust particle?

Or, are you, as a human being – the only being endowed with the faculty of thinking – aware of the perfect order existing in the universe?

There are surely hundreds of similar questions you could ask yourself. The purpose in mentioning these questions is to unveil – albeit slightly – the covering over the human mind, which is already obscured by daily tasks, and help to expand its horizons. Our intention here is to reflect on some crucial issues.

Now, consider the following:

"What is the significance of these questions for my life? Is it really important to think about them while I have hundreds of things to accomplish? My final examinations... the meeting that will be held in late afternoon... don't they have priority?"

These thoughts reflect a common mistake many people make. No doubt, plans pertaining to one's education, home or future are important. Yet there are some issues which are more important. Primarily, a person should reflect on the purpose of his existence in this world, on what exists beyond this life, on how this magnificent planet on which he lives came into existence, and on who is the Creator of all living things, including him.

From the moment man wakes in the morning, he has to involve himself in endless pursuits. However, in the middle of all these mundane incidents, he doesn't think much about a VERY IMPORTANT issue: man occupies an almost insignificant space in the whole universe, similar to the volume of a building a dust particle occupies. It may be astonishing to realise, yet, this is an OBVIOUS fact.

If one thinks earnestly without pretending not to grasp the facts one comes across, one would arrive at a single conclusion:

In the immense universe, an astonishing variety of plants and animals, all beings – animate or inanimate – and more importantly man himself, are parts of the flawless creation of Allah, the Almighty. Man doesn't see his Creator, yet, pondering on the countless pieces of evidence surrounding him will make him comprehend Allah's existence and His attributes. In his efforts, his sincerity will provide him with a way to understanding his Creator's commandments and the ways to attaining His good pleasure. Allah relates in the Qur'an:

> Eyesight cannot perceive Him but He perceives eyesight. He is the All-Penetrating, the All-Aware. Clear insights have come to you from your Lord. Whoever sees clearly, does so to his own benefit. Whoever is blind, it is to his own detriment. I am not here as your keeper. (Surat al-An'am: 103-104)

You also reflect on this fact and never pretend you don't grasp the superior creation of Allah.

People are so immersed in the daily flow of their lives that they cannot realise the miraculous conditions on which their lives rest. However, for a man of understanding, the fact that he lives on a sphere spinning on its axis at a speed of 1670 kilometres an hour means a lot. Moreover, that this sphere is favoured with delicate balances to make life possible indicates that this flawless system is the product of an OBVIOUS act of creation, the creation of ALLAH THE ALMIGHTY. So don't pretend not to grasp this fact of which we remind you, and be grateful to your Creator since He created you and gave you a soul.

Never Plead Ignorance

About the Obvious Existence of Allah

*F*rom the moment man opens his eyes to this world a great order surrounds him. He needs oxygen to survive. It is interesting that the atmosphere of the planet on which he lives provides more than just the adequate amount of oxygen he needs. This way, he breathes without difficulty. For the existence of life on this planet, the existence of a source of heat is essential. In response to this need, the sun is located just at the right distance to emit just the exact amount of heat and energy man needs. Man needs nourishment to survive. Every corner of the world abounds in astonishingly diversified provisions. Likewise, man needs water. Surprisingly, three-fourths of the planet is covered with water. Man needs shelter, and in this world, there is land on which it is suitable to build and all sorts of materials to make shelters.

These are only a few among billions of details making life possible on earth. In brief, man lives on a planet perfectly designed for his survival. This is certainly a planet "created for human beings".

A person's interpretation of the world rests on "acquired methods of thought." That is, he thinks in the way he has been taught, or, less kindly, the way in which he is indoctrinated. Under this misguidance, he often dismisses all the aforementioned as "trivial realities." However, if he does not side-step the matter, and start questioning the conditions making our existence possible, he will surely step out of the boundaries of habitual thinking and start to think:

How does the atmosphere serve as a protective ceiling for the earth?

How does each one of the billions of cells in the human body know and perform its individual tasks?

How does this extraordinary ecological balance exist on earth?

A person seeking answers to these questions surely proceeds on the right path. He does not remain insensitive to things happening around him, and doesn't plead ignorance about the extraordinary nature of the world. A person who asks questions, who reflects on and gives answers to these questions will realise that on every inch of the planet, a plan and an order reigns:

How did the flawless order in the whole universe come into being?

Who provided the delicate balances in the world?

How did living beings, incredibly diversified in nature, emerge?

Keeping oneself occupied with relentless research to answer these questions results in a clear awareness that everything in the universe, its order, each living being and structure is a component of a plan, a product of design. Every detail, the excellent structure of an insect's wing, the system enabling a tree to carry tons of water to its topmost branches, the order of planets, and the ratio of gases in the atmosphere, are all unique examples of perfection.

In every detail of the infinitely varied world, man finds his Creator. Allah, the owner of everything in the whole universe, introduces Himself to man through the flawless design of His creation. Everything surrounding us, the birds in flight, our beating hearts, the birth of a child or the existence of the sun in the sky, manifest the power of Allah and His creation. And what man must do is to understand this fact.

These purposes owe their existence to the fact that everything has been created. An intelligent person notices that plan, design and wisdom exist in every detail of the infinitely varied world. This draws him to recognition of the Creator.

So you never plead ignorance that all living beings, living or non-living, show the existence and greatness of Allah. Look at things around you and strive to show appreciation in the best manner for the

eternal greatness of Allah.

The existence of Allah is OBVIOUS. Ignoring it would only be the beginning of the greatest damage we could ever do to ourselves. That is simply because Allah is in no need of anything. He is the One Who shows His greatness in all things and in all ways. Allah is the owner of everything, from the heavens to the earth. We learn the attributes of Allah from the Qur'an:

> Allah! There is no god but Him, the Living, the Self-Sustaining. He is not subject to drowsiness or sleep. Everything in the heavens and the earth belongs to Him. Who can intercede with Him except by His permission? He knows what is before them and what is behind them but they cannot grasp any of His knowledge save what He wills. His Footstool encompasses the heavens and the earth and their preservation does not tire Him. He is the Most High, the Magnificent. (Surat al-Baqarah: 255)

Never Plead Ignorance

that Evolution is a Deceit and Allah Creates Everything

R eluctant to acknowledge the existence of Allah, some people advanced a "theory of coincidences" about how life came into existence. This implausible theory, wholly contradicting scientific evidence, suggests that all living beings on earth came into existence as a result of random chance. However, an examination of these groundless claims reveals that this theory brings not one single rational explanation about "how life came into existence."

A close look at the flawless systems inherent in living beings eventually leads us to one obvious fact: all living beings are created. All evolutionist claims regarding the origin of life are wholly invalid. A process called evolution has never occurred on earth. The Creator created the universe in its unique form, and evolution is a hoax. These are the facts.

Despite the fact that all scientific and reasonable evidence pertaining to the origin of life obviously indicates its CREATION, some people still insistently advocate evolution. In this chapter, we will review how some people, claiming to be adherents of science, assert such irrational claims. We will also witness how this theory, to which people are blindly attached, has collapsed by means of the major breakthroughs in science made in the 20th century.

Never make the mistake that these people did, who are making furious efforts to reject the existence of Allah. Never plead ignorance of the fact that everything is the creation of Allah and that a process called evolution never occurred on earth.

● Evolutionists claim that living beings evolve through two main mechanisms: "Mutation" and "Natural Selection".

According to evolutionists, a reason for evolutionary change is random mutations occurring in the genetic structure of living beings. They claim that consecutive little mutations create new species. Yet, mutations only cause damage to the DNA, the structure in which all the information pertaining to the cell is coded. The effects of mutations are always harmful and it is implausible that mutation leads to the formation of a new species. All the mutations that we know of that take place in humans result in physical deformities, in infirmities such as mongolism, albinism, dwarfism or cancer. The people exposed to the radiation of the nuclear weapons dropped on Hiroshima and Nagasaki in the recent past are concrete examples of the mutations occurring in living beings due to radiation.

Natural selection holds that those living things that are more suited to the natural conditions of their habitats will prevail by having offspring that will survive, whereas those that are unfit will disappear. However, this claim has no relation to any evolutionary process. Natural selection only weeds out the weak individuals of a species and accordingly lead to a society made up of strong individuals. In other words, natural selection cannot produce new species.

Evolutionists are also aware of this fact. Colin Patterson, senior palaeontologist of the Museum of Natural History in England, stresses that natural selection has never been observed to have the power to make things evolve:

> No one has ever produced a species by mechanisms of natural selection. No one has ever got near it and most of the current argument in neo-Darwinism is about this question.

So, never plead ignorance that neither of the mechanisms, behind which evolutionists hide, are magic wands that transform living organisms into more advanced and perfect forms.

● According to the theory of evolution, every living species has sprung from a predecessor. Yet, if this was the case, then numerous intermediary species should have existed and lived within this long period of transformation. In other words, some half-fish, half-reptile creatures should have lived in the past, exhibiting some reptilian traits in addition to the fish traits they already had. Evolutionists refer to these imaginary creatures, which they believe to have lived in the past, as "transitional forms."

If such animals had really existed, there should have been millions and even billions of them. More importantly, the remains of these strange creatures should be present in the fossil record. Yet, to our surprise, extensive research concluded that in the fossil records these "transitional links" were missing. Fossil records pertaining to other living beings are quite rich whereas not a single fossil of these imaginary beings is present.

So, never plead ignorance that the absence of transitional forms invalidates evolutionist claims.

● According to the imaginary scenario of evolutionists, some fish felt the necessity to pass from sea to land for various reasons. Upon this need (!), some changes occurred in the fish, transforming them in time into amphibians. This is a brief summary of the evolutionary scenario arguing the transition from water to land. Now, let's consider this for a moment. What happens if fish one day decide to pass on to the land? Do fish, gradually approaching the coast, and finally reaching the sand, have a chance of survival? The answer is clear: fish moving on to the land would soon die. Other fish attempting to do the same would also die. The result would still be the same if billions of fish tried to do the same for millions of years: each fish reaching the land would die before having the opportunity to do anything. This is an OBVIOUS fact.

Besides, today it is scientifically shown that it is unlikely for these living beings, differing greatly from each other anatomically and physiologically, to have evolved from each other. There are a number of obvious facts that render such a transition impossible.

The drawing above, the so-called transformation of starfish into fish, is a mere figment of imagination. There are numerous fossils both of the starfish and fish seen in this arrangement, yet, the imaginary creature that is half starfish, half fish is only a drawing. These drawings of alleged transitional forms have no evidence in the fossil record.

1. Carrying weight: land-dwelling creatures consume 40% of their energy just carrying their bodies around. Sea-dwelling creatures, however, have no problem in carrying their own weights. Land-dwelling and sea-dwelling creatures have completely different muscular and skeletal systems and hence are perfectly adapted to their environments.

2. Retention of heat: a land-dwelling creature has a bodily mechanism that can withstand great temperature fluctuations on land. However, in the sea, the temperature changes slowly and the change does not occur within such a wide range. That is why the metabolisms of land-dwelling and sea-dwelling creatures differ greatly. The chance that such a transition occurs coincidentally is truly unlikely.

3. Use of Water: essential to metabolism, water and moisture need to be used restrictively due to scarce sources of water on land. For instance, the skin is designed to permit loss of water to a certain extent while also preventing excessive evaporation. Land-dwelling creatures have a sense of thirst, something that sea-dwelling organisms do not have. Besides, the skins of sea-creatures are not suitable for a non-aquatic habitat.

4. Kidneys: sea-creatures can easily discharge waste materials in their bodies by filtering them, since there is plenty of water in their habitat. However, on land water has to be used economically. This is why land creatures have a kidney system. It is improbable that the kidney, a complex structure, comes into existence coincidentally.

What happens to a fish if one day it crosses on to the land? This is surely something that is imagined by people without giving it thought. Claiming that a fish remained on land for decades without dying and one day decided to live as a reptile is surely unreasonable and unscientific.

5. Respiratory System: fish breathe by taking in oxygen dissolved in water that they pass through their gills. Land-dwelling animals, on the other hand, have a complete lung system.

Fish have always been fish and reptiles have always been reptiles. So, never plead ignorance of the fact that fish can never evolve into snakes or lizards, and that such a scenario can only be narrated in stories.

● Unable to explain how the perfect structure of bird feathers occurred, evolutionists claim that birds evolved from reptiles. This is surely a groundless claim. The fossil record reveals that birds have always been birds and reptiles have always been reptiles.

Due to several physiological and anatomical differences, such a transition is implausible. To cite a few examples;

- Birds have a totally different lung structure from reptiles.

- Their skeletal structure is totally different from reptiles; for instance the bones of birds are lighter than the bones of reptiles.

- Birds have feathers, whereas reptiles are covered with scales.

An imaginary drawing: dinosaurs that suddenly took wing while trying to catch flies.

In brief, the scenarios that the forelegs of a reptile transformed into wings and that then they started flying has no scientific basis whatsoever. Never plead ignorance of the fact that a reptile can never transform into a bird.

● Another fact invalidates the theory of evolution. Evolutionists fail to bring an explanation of how life originated on earth.

All living beings are made up of cells. For instance, there are 100 trillion cells in a human organism. Proteins are the basic building blocks of the cell. The formation, under natural conditions, of but one single protein, out of the thousands of complex protein molecules making up the cell, is not possible.

Proteins are giant molecules consisting of smaller units called "amino-acids", the simplest of which is composed of 50 amino acids, but there are some that are composed of thousands of amino acids. The crucial point is that the absence, addition, or replacement of a single amino in the structure of a protein would transform it into a useless molecular heap. Every amino acid has to be at the right place and in the right order.

The fact that the functional structure of proteins absolutely cannot come about by chance can easily be understood even from simple probability calculations that anybody can understand.

An average sized protein molecule is composed of 288 amino acids of which there are twelve different types. These can be arranged in 10^{300}

different ways. In other words, the probability of the formation of only one protein molecule is "1 out of 10^{300} ". The probability of this "1" to occur is therefore practically impossible.

So, never plead ignorance of the fact that it is implausible for proteins, the building blocks of the cell, to occur through chance and that consequently life could not have originated as alleged by evolutionists.

● If the coincidental formation of even one of these proteins is impossible, it is billions of times more impossible for about one million of those proteins to come together properly by chance and make up a complete human cell.

Robert Shapiro, professor of chemistry at New York University and a DNA expert, calculated the probability of the coincidental formation of the 200 types of proteins found in single bacteria. (There are 200,000 different types of proteins in a human cell) The number that was found was 1 over $10^{40.000}$. [1]

A professor of applied mathematics and astronomy from University College (Cardiff, Wales), Chandra Wickramasinghe, comments on this incredible probability:

> The likelihood of the spontaneous formation of life from inanimate matter is one to a number with 40.000 noughts after it... it is big enough to bury Darwin and the whole theory of evolution. There was no primeval soup, either on this planet or on any other, and if the beginning of life was not by chance, it must therefore have been the creation of purposeful intelligence. [2]

So, never plead ignorance of the fact that even a single bacteria could not have come into existence coincidentally or by accident. That implies the collapse of the theory of evolution.

● The molecule called DNA, which is found in the nucleus of each of the 100 trillion cells in our body, contains the complete construction plan of the human body. Information regarding all characteristics of a person, from physical appearance to the structure of the internal organs, is en-

Is it probable that all the information compiled in thousands of books in a library is written by chance? The answer is "No". So, it is evident that DNA, the molecule in which all the information of a living being is stored, cannot come into existence by chance.

coded in the DNA by means of a special system. If we were to write down the information encoded in DNA, then we would need to compile a giant library consisting of 900 encyclopædic volumes of 500 pages each.

This incredibly voluminous information is encoded in the components of DNA called "genes". At this point, there is an important detail that deserves attention. An error in the sequence of nucleotides making up a gene would render the gene completely useless. When we consider that there are 200 thousand genes in the human body, it becomes more evident how impossible it is for the millions of nucleotides making up these genes to be formed in the right sequence by coincidence.

So, never plead ignorance of the fact that this complex structure of DNA is a special design. This is concrete evidence that DNA is created by Allah.

● Evolutionists assert that all living beings evolved from the primitive forms to the advanced. According to this groundless assertion, human beings, too, evolved from half-man, half-ape beings called "primitive human beings". However, today we know that there is not a concept of "primitive man." Men have always been men and apes have always been apes. This is a fact that has been proved. Fossils, alleged to be the ancestors of men, belong to human races that lived until very recently – about 10,000 years ago – and then disappeared. Moreover, many human communities currently living have the same physical appearance and characteristics as these extinct human races, which the evolutionists claim to be pre-human ancestors of men.

There are numerous anatomical differences between apes and men and none of them are of the kind to come into existence through an evolutionary process. This is an OBVIOUS fact.

A few examples indicating this are the following:

In 1995, an 800 thousand-year-old human face fossil was found in Atapuerca, Spain. This fossil is important in the sense that it is no different from modern man. This reveals an undeniable fact: the human beings who lived 800,000 years ago and modern man are the same.

· - An item published in *New Scientist* on March 14th 1998 tells us that humans called by evolutionists Homo Erectus were practising seamanship 700 thousand years ago. These humans who had enough knowledge and technology to build a vessel and possess a culture that made use of

What Happens to a Car Left in the Desert for a Decade?
The Second Law of Thermodynamics, which is accepted as one of the basic laws of physics, holds that under normal conditions, all systems left on their own will tend to become disordered, dispersed, and corrupted to an extent that is in direct relation to the amount of time that passes. In our daily lives, we also observe that everything, animate or inanimate, wears out, deteriorates, decays, disintegrates, and is destroyed. For instance, if we leave a car in the desert and then check up on it after months, we would hardly expect to find it in a better condition. On the contrary, we would find that its tyres were flat, its windows broken, its chassis rusted and its motor non-functional. The theory of evolution, however, says that disordered, dispersed, and inorganic atoms and molecules spontaneously come together in time in a certain order and plan to form extremely complex structures. This is another contradictory and unscientific point of view of evolutionary theory.

An item published in the *New Scientist* on March 14th 1998 tells us that the species called by evolutionists Homo Erectus were practising seamanship 700 thousand years ago.

THIS WEEK

Ancient mariners

Early humans were much smarter than we suspected

OUR ancestors made organised sea journeys more than 700 000 years earlier than previously thought—and they probably used language to coordinate their efforts.

This surprising new theory comes from palaeoanthropologist Mike Morwood and his colleagues at the University of New England in northern New South Wales. It is the result of an intriguing find during their exploration of an ancient lake bed at Mata Menge on the island of

ash surrounding the tools were between 800 000 and 880 000 years old. Fossil plants and animals found near the tools dated from the same period.

The researchers believe the tools were used by the ancestral human species *Homo*

sea transport, can hardly be called primitive.

- Near Lake Turkana, Kenya, a fossil of a child with an upright skeletal structure has been found which is no different from that of modern man. Concerning this fossil of a Homo Erectus specimen, paleoanthropologists share a common view. American paleontologist Alan Walker stated that he doubted that "the average pathologist could tell the difference between the fossil skeleton and that of a modern human."[3]

- Neanderthals were a human race yet evolutionists present them as "a primitive species." Nevertheless, all findings, including a sewing needle fossil dated 26 thousand years belonging to this race testify that Neanderthals, ten thousands of years ago, had knowledge of clothing.

Never plead ignorance of the fact that these men, who lived hundreds of thousands of years ago, practised seamanship and had knowledge of clothing, and had a skeletal structure no different from modern man, are presented as "primitive men" and that these efforts are vain.

● About the origin of man, evolutionists arrange ape-like "transitional forms" and call the resulting sequence "the imaginary family tree of man." According to evolutionists, the origin of man was from an ape who later acquired the traits of man.

This family tree of man is completely imaginary. To have a better understanding of the imaginary nature of this arrangement, it is sufficient to examine evolutionists' alleged basis for this story.

Sometimes a skull, jaw-bone or single tooth has been the spark of inspiration for evolutionists to arrange these "transitional forms." Relying on a bone, it is nevertheless not possible to picture the physical appearance of a living being, and certainly not the family tree of the same living being. That is however exactly what evolutionists dare to do. Relying on a single bone, they put forth imaginary yet quite detailed scenarios about living beings and from them form family trees.

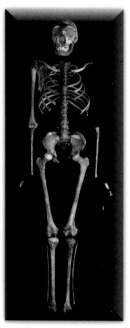

"Turkana Boy" fossil that belongs to the Homo Erectus race. Almost no different from modern man.

Apart from these imaginary family trees, evolutionists develop incomprehensible scenarios from a single bone. For instance, pictures of ape-like men with their ape-like spouses and children sitting next to a fire have been published in various publications for decades. These publications are all products of evolutionists' subjective interpretation. This is the way to indoctrinate people into believing the existence of half-ape, half-human creatures in history. Detailed pictures depicting these imaginary creatures walking with their families, hunting, or in other moments of their daily lives are surely figments of the imagination and have no counterpart in the fossil record.

So far, we have examined that the theory of evolution has no scientific ground. Yet, there is another fact that is more obvious than the rest. This OBVIOUS fact is the following:

The living being we call "the human being" is a composition of atoms of phosphate, magnesium, carbon and calcium, among others. These atoms have no individual will or conscience. Yet, to our surprise, these inanimate atoms come together to form a living human being. Moreover, this "composition of atoms" decided to attend a university, make a career and become, say, a professor. This professor, made up of atoms, decided to be an expert on microbiology and examine his own cell structure under the electron microscope. He may have decided to become an expert on medicine and treat diseases caused by viruses, also made up of atoms.

This is what evolutionists assert. They know exactly that the atom has no consciousness, yet, they further claim that atoms are assembled into beings which have feelings and which think.

Man is a being who has will and consciousness. He takes decisions, speaks and arrives at conclusions. All these features and functions of the "soul" make man different.

Never PLEAD IGNORANCE of the fact that even if all the parts making up a person could come together coincidentally, such a heap of atoms would not form the "spirit."

Never Plead Ignorance

About The Miraculous Features of Living Beings Surrounding You

*A*s is dealt with in depth in the previous sections of this book, it is evident that it is not possible to say that even a single cell came into existence by coincidence. Let's consider the following then: since even a single cell could not have come into existence by chance, is it possible to say that a variety of living beings came into existence by coincidence? The answer is certainly "No."

Have you ever thought about the variety of living beings surrounding you? Let's think about all the plants we see in books, or in documentary series on television, all the carnations, roses, daisies, water lilies, giant tropical plants, pineapples, acacia trees. Let's remember their individual leaf structures, tastes, colours, scents, the methods of photosynthesis

they employ, and all other details pertaining to them.

Let's also consider animals; let's think about giraffes, antelopes, elephants, chickens, all types of fish, sparrows, peacocks, ostriches, rabbits, butterflies, and various insects. Let's think about their mechanisms, their habitats, and the way they hunt or reproduce.

Even such brief reflection would make us realise the variety of living beings on the earth on which we live.

There are 200 thousand butterfly species on earth. Furthermore, naturalists have found that these species embody 1 million types of butterflies, all having highly complex and remarkable individual systems which employ amazing camouflage techniques. Some, for instance, imitate a leaf to protect themselves from their enemies. Others, on the other hand, have eye-shaped patterns on their wings for the same purpose.

Consider the variety of these remarkable designs, and never PLEAD IGNORANCE of the fact that millions of living-beings, each so unique in their design, could not have evolved from each other.

A person who makes a conscious effort to understand the miraculous attributes of living beings would easily find the answer to the question "how did these beings emerge?" Allah furnishes all living beings with extraordinary features and shows men the evident signs of His existence and might.

Never PLEAD IGNORANCE of this obvious fact that is so easy to see.

He is the Originator of the heavens and the earth. How could He have a son when He has no wife? He created all things and He has knowledge of all things. That is Allah, your Lord! There is no god but Him, the Creator of everything. So worship Him. He is responsible for everything. (Surat al-An'am: 101-102)

Apart from this variety, a number of living beings in nature are equipped with astonishing systems and complex mechanisms by which they perform complicated tasks. These are actually tasks that are not even accomplished by human beings. The extraordinary designs that prevail in these mechanisms can by no means be explained by chance, as the theory of evolution suggests. Each living being is designed specially thus enabling it to survive in its particular habitat. It is unlikely that living beings could design these systems themselves. These flawless systems are inherent in their creation.

In this section, we will review only a few of these miraculous mechanisms observed in plants and animals.

While reading these examples, ponder deeply, and never PLEAD IGNORANCE of the fact that these mechanisms are so perfect that they could not have come into existence by themselves.

When we say "the flawless structures of animals", some people may think that we are talking about the interesting attributes of as yet unheard, uncommon living beings. However, everyone is familiar with the attributes we are talking about. There is great design in the body of an insect or a tiny bird. This design is so complex that, so far, no human being has ever accomplished the production of such a design. An attentive eye would have no difficulty in recognising that this design, which is obvious in all nature, provides solid evidence of creation.

For instance, it takes an enormous amount of energy for a fly to fly. That is why the fly has an entirely different respiratory system. Special, fine air tubes in their bodies directly transmit oxygen in the air to the cells, enabling the rapid combustion of oxygen. This, however, is only one of the miraculous attributes of a fly. Allah draws our attention to the superior design evident in the creation of fly:

The extraordinary design discernible in the wing of a fly, flapping its wings 500 times a second.

Mankind! an example has been made, so listen to it carefully. Those whom you call upon besides Allah are not even able to create a single fly, even if they were to join together to do it. And if a fly steals something from them, they cannot get it back. How feeble are both the seeker and the sought! (Surat al-Hajj: 73)

Let's consider bees. Everyone is familiar with the social nature of bees or the hexagonal structure of honeycomb. However, the attributes of bees are not limited to these alone. Care for the hive is an essential part of the bee's life. Worker bees control the temperature, and manage the security and cleaning of the hive. Whatever the temperature outside, honey-

Bees working to-keep the heat of the hive at a constant temperature.

bees keep the temperature of the of the hive - especially the brood chamber - constant. In the chill of early morning, workers cluster over the comb, incubating the brood with body heat. As the day warms, the tightly knit cluster gradually disperses. If the temperature continues to climb, some of the workers begin to fan their wings, directing a cooling flow of air through the hive entrance and over the combs. On an extremely hot day, the bees must resort to an even more drastic cooling measure: They place drops of dilute honey at the openings of empty cells, evaporating the liquid in the airstream created by their wings. This cooling system reduces the hive temperature dramatically. If, however, there is still not enough fresh, unconcentrated honey on hand, the foragers begin to scout for water.[4]

Flawless conscious design is inherent in the living beings surrounding us. The attributes mentioned here are no doubt only a small part of their extraordinary features. These are evident signs for people of understanding of Allah's existence and of His might.

Nevertheless, the majority of people never think about these or they ignore the miraculous attributes of living beings. **Yet, NEVER PLEAD IGNORANCE about the superior creation and the unique art of Allah.**

The superiority and uniqueness of the creation of Allah are also displayed in living beings that we do not observe. A striking example is the Sybrian salamander. These living beings can remain in the depths of frozen soil for years and return to their ordinary way of living when weather conditions improve and the ice melts. These salamanders can survive even at -50° C, thanks to an anti-freeze-like material produced in

Fireflies, excelling modern technology, with their inherent systems.

their bodies protecting them against freezing cold. This anti-freeze material replaces water in blood cells, preventing the tissues from damage caused by ice-crystals.[5]

There is an important feature of the light emitted by fireflies: this light has no heat, a condition called "cold light." In today's world, this would be considered a major technological breakthrough and is largely thought unattainable. An ordinary bulb transforms only 3-4% of its electrical energy into light. The remainder is transformed into heat. Fireflies, however, transform 100% of its energy into light, without the dissipation of any in the form of heat.[6]

Diving tanks in a submarine filled with water make the submarine heavier than water, enabling it to sink to the bottom of the ocean. If water in the tank is emptied by pressurised air, the submarine floats again. Nautilus, a marine animal, also employs exactly the same method. A spiral organ shaped like a snail shell, and 19 cm in diameter, Nautilus embodies 28 interconnected "diving cells". How does Nautilus, then, find the pressurised air necessary to expel the water? Hard to believe, but Nautilus, through biochemical means, produces a special gas, which is conveyed to the cells through its bloodstream. This gas eventually expels the water in the cells. Nautilus pumps out the amount of water necessary to sink or float and hence performs essential functions like hunting or protecting itself against its enemies. A submarine dives to 400 metres while a

Nautilus, an interesting marine animal.

Nautilus can dive to 4,000 metres.[7]

It is actually not man who invented cooling systems. Every warm-blooded living being possesses various mechanisms for temperature control. The gazelle, a fast running African animal, must often sprint to protect itself against its enemies. Such effort raises the body temperature. However, to survive, it is essential that the gazelle should keep its brain cool.

For this purpose, the gazelle has its own cooling system built right into its head. Gazelles have hundreds of small arteries that divide and pass through a large pool of blood lying next to its breathing passages. Air taken in by the animal cools this nasal pool, so the blood passing through the tiny arteries in it is cooled, too. Then, the tiny arteries come together in a single blood vessel that carries blood to the brain. In the absence of such a system, the gazelle simply could not survive.[8]

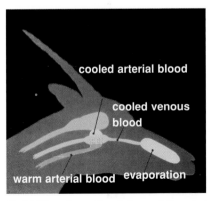

cooled arterial blood

cooled venous blood

warm arterial blood   evaporation

(Left) The shematic picture of the skeletal structure of gazelle. (Right) A gazelle prepared to escape its enemy.

Hunting birds have keen eyes that enable them to locate their prey and protect themselves against them. Yet in this sense, no hunting bird is better equipped than the owl. Some species turn their heads through one hundred degrees, an ability very useful for extending the angle of vision of the owl's eyes.

No doubt, the most remarkable feature of the owl's eyes is their size. These big eyes cover a considerable part of the face and are separated only by a thin bone. The eyes rest tightly in the eye cavity and leave almost no room for muscles. They are unable to move and force the owl to use its flexible neck and turn in different directions.[9]

Once the owl locates its prey's position, it should lose no time in attacking it. However, the majority of birds make noise while flying. The noise of the wings of an eagle, for instance, can be heard miles away, as can the wings of many other big birds. Noisy wings are obviously disadvantageous for a night hunter. However, the owl's soft feathers with their tassel-like structures at the ends allow the owl to fly noiselessly. The surface of the wings' velvet-soft feathers efficiently absorbs noise.[10]

Rattlesnakes are able to locate warm-blooded animals – a rat, for instance – even in pitch darkness. The rattlesnake can still sense a rat only 15cm away, although the rat causes a minor temperature change of only 0.005°C. Information regarding the prey is conveyed to the brain, assessed and responded to by the snake in less than

Rattlesnakes, with their eyes sensitive to heat, can see warm-blooded animals even in pitch darkness.

1/20th of a second. When we consider that one second is just as long as the blink of an eye, the incredible speed of the snake is better understood. The rattlesnake, finding the location of its prey without error, attacks and kills it with its poisonous teeth.[11]

Sea otters comb their fur with their feet, a method they employ to clean and groom their fur with the oil made in their skin. This operation is a unique way of airing the fur since it enables tiny bubbles of air to be trapped by the thick underfur. In the freezing cold of the Pacific, the air bubble-holding capacity of the fur has an essential role in the perfect adaptation the sea otter has to unfavourable weather conditions. These bubbles simply protect sea otters against freezing. Matting of the sea otter's hair – usually caused by fuel waste products – simply means death.[12]

The Wedel seal can survive in the freezing waters of the Antarctic, even when the temperature drops below –26°C. It is not affected by intense and sudden changes of pressure when it dives to the bottom of the ocean, since before a deep dive, the seal makes several short dives. Opening and closing its rib bones and diaphragm, it lets out the air in its lungs and closes its lungs. After a while, when no air is left in the lungs, nitrogen does not dissolve and loses all possibility of entering the bloodstream. This is a process that enables the animal to survive. Contrary to the majority of mammals, seals have a flat oval-shaped trachea, rather than a round one, which easily closes under high pressure. Such a structure grants the seal perfect adaptation to its environment.[13]

During the day, the heart of a hummingbird beats between 500 and 1,200 times a second. In the evening, its heartbeat slows down so much that its throb is virtually undetectable. Nor does the bird

A sea otter, protecting itself against the freezing cold of the Pacific by a special method.

A Hummingbird.

appear to be breathing. In effect, it is doing what a hedgehog does when winter approaches. It is hibernating. The hummingbird, however, has to hibernate 365 times every year.[14]

These are only a few examples of the divergence of living beings. However, these examples are enough to reveal the design inherent in them. It is unlikely that these elaborate systems could have occurred by chance. Coincidences have no consciousness; they can devise no plans. All these living beings are surely the product of conscious design. This flawless design is only one of the signs showing that all living beings are created. Allah, the Sustainer of all the worlds, granted these attributes to them. A subtle art and wisdom are displayed in His creation.

So, NEVER PLEAD IGNORANCE of the fact that these miraculous systems are only products of the superior creation of Allah.

Take a plant and look at its leaves closely. Examine the arrangement of its leaves, and its colour and brightness. Just consider how leaves of the top branches of trees hundreds of metres above sea-level remain green all year round? Then, turn and look at birds flying in the sky. Take a feather and analyse it under a microscope. Such an analysis reveals that birds' feathers are made up of thousands of tiny tendrils attached to one another by hooks.

Analysis of various other living beings makes us arrive at the same conclusion: a detailed design is evident in all living beings. How did these feathers come into existence? Is it possible that these complex designs can be attributed to blind chance and coincidences?

Let's provide the answers to these questions by asking other ques-

Even the unique design of the feather is an indication of creation.

tions. Is it possible for a plane to be constructed without conscious intervention? Alternatively, does a random arrangement of tiles make up a factory? The answer is obvious. Technological products supported by highly complex structures are designed and produced by intelligent men. Similarly, the flawless design observable in nature is the end product of an exalted Creator. This is an OBVIOUS fact.

Pierre Grasse, a prominent French zoologist and the former president of the French Sciences Academy states the following:

> A single plant, a single animal would require thousands and thousands of lucky, appropriate events. Thus, miracles would become the rule: events with an infinitessimal probability could not fail to occur. There is no law against daydreaming, but science must not indulge in it.[15]

The thought that living organisms could come into existence by chance is only a figment of the imagination.

LIVING BEINGS DID NOT COME INTO EXISTENCE BY CHANCE. Allah, the Sustainer of the worlds, creates all of them. So, NEVER PLEAD IGNORANCE of this obvious fact, which today must be comprehensible to everybody.

The wisdom, design and order we observe in nature prevail throughout the universe. From the world we live in to all the heavenly bodies in space, there is a flawless planning.

Our world is perfectly orderly. Countless billions of systems function simultaneously yet in total harmony. There is an incredible equilibrium within this gigantic network of systems, which reveals that life on earth, which rests on a delicate system of balances, is specially designed. A comparison between other planets in the solar system and the earth would show this fact better. The earth is the only planet in the solar system which supports life.

The delicate balances inherent in the planet make this possible. The velocity of the earth's rotation about its axis is one of them. These delicate balances make the earth a habitable place. For instance, the atmosphere of the earth consists of gases in ideal proportions for the survival of man as well as all other living beings (77% nitrogen, 21% oxygen and 1% carbon dioxide and other gases). Let's take one of these gases, oxygen, for instance. If the ratio of oxygen to the other gases were a little higher than 21%, the cells of living beings would be severely damaged. Moreover, the molecules of hydro-carbons and thus plants would also have no chance of existing.

If the proportion of oxygen to other gases were a little less, than breathing would be torture. Furthermore, the transformation of nutriments into energy would become impossible. Similarly, if the proportion of carbon dioxide in the air were greater, it would pose a threat to mankind since the atmosphere would keep more heat, increasing the overall temperature of the earth. A slight decrease in the amount of carbon dioxide, on the other hand, would cause great temperature differences between day and night, with the temperature falling below zero at nights. The proportion of nitrogen in the air is so delicate that oxygen, a flammable gas, acquires a vital importance for living beings.

The constant nature of atmospheric gases is another important factor for life. Plants produce around 200 billion tons of oxygen a year by transforming the carbon dioxide in the air into oxygen.

The mass of the earth, too, is ideal, and prevents the atmosphere drifting out into space.

With regard to these balances in the atmosphere, it is essential that the temperature of the surface of the earth should be relatively constant. This constancy is closely related to the regularity of the orbit that the earth follows around the sun, the size of the sun, the velocity of rotation of the earth and the inclination of the earth's axis.

There are various other balances that enable earth to support life.

The current power of the gravitational force exhibits a delicate balance. A slight increase in the gravitational force, would mean more ammonia and methane in the atmosphere, which would be detrimental to life. In the contrary situation, however, the atmosphere would fail to hold water, changing the world into an uninhabitable place.

The thickness of the earth's crust and the ozone layer, the water and nitrogen cycles on earth, the existence of mountains, the protective nature of the atmospheric layers are essential for the continuance of life.

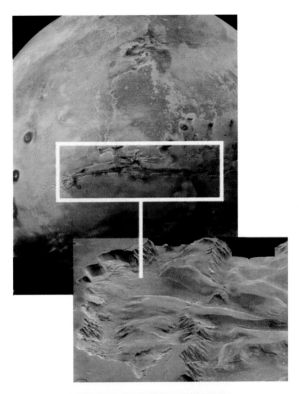

The only planet supporting life in the solar system is the Earth. A section from the planet Mars (above). A comparison between other planets and the earth would make man feel the astonishing design inherent in this planet.

The majority of people, however, lead lives having no idea of the delicate balances of the composition of gases in the atmosphere, the distance of the earth from the sun or the movements of the planets. The vital importance of such balances do not mean much to them. However, even a subtle change in one of these balances would become a major threat to the continuance of life. Furthermore, the above-mentioned are only a few among billions of delicate balances existing on earth. However, it is an OBVIOUS fact that even these are enough to show that they are all the products of a superior wisdom.

So, NEVER PLEAD IGNORANCE of the fact that such delicate balances could not have occurred by chance, and that only Allah the Almighty has the power to establish such an order.

Life on earth exists on the "crust" of the earth, a section of 7 layers with a distance of 670 km. The crust, 6,370 km deep, makes up only 1% of the depth of this section. Scientists, drawing an analogy between an apple and the world, state that the outer part of an apple is similar to the crust of the earth whereon life exists, whereas the inner part of the apple is similar to the planet's interior, an inner core of molten elements. Just considering that 12km below the earth the temperature is about 60°C shows that the world is anything but serene and still. Possessions, children, career, and people's possessions, all belong to a life led on top of this core of molten elements.

MAGNETIC FIELD

MANTLE

CRUST

OUTER CORE

INNER CORE

Never Plead Ignorance

that Everything You Possess is a Favour From Allah

*I*n the world in which we live, Allah bestows many favours on man. All the needs of each living being are benevolently met; no detail is forgotten.

Let's think about ourselves as examples. From the moment we wake in the morning, we need many things and encounter many situations. In brief, we survive due to the many favours bestowed upon us.

We can breathe as soon as we wake up. We never experience difficulty in doing this, thanks to our respiratory systems functioning perfectly.

We can see as soon as we open our eyes. The sharp and distant images, all three-dimensional and fully coloured, are perceived by our eyes, and indeed owe their existence to the unique design of eyes.

We taste delicious flavours. The relative proportions of the vitamin, mineral, carbohydrate or protein content of the food we eat, or how the excess of these nutrients are stored or utilised in the body never concern us. Moreover, we are mostly never aware that such complicated operations take place in our body.

When we hold some material in our hands, we immediately know if it is soft or hard. What is more, we need no mental effort to do this. Numerous similar minute operations take place in our body. The organs, responsible for these operations, have complicated mechanisms. The human body functions almost like a factory of enormous complexity and ingenuity. This body is one of the major favours given to man since man leads his existence on earth with it.

At this point, a question remains to be answered: how are the raw materials necessary to operate this factory supplied? To put it another way, how do water, air, and all the other nutrients essential for life come into existence?

Let's think about fruits and vegetables. Melons, watermelons, cherries, oranges, tomatoes, peppers, pineapples, mulberries, grapes, eggplants... all grow in soil from seeds, and the seed has a structure sometimes as hard as wood. However, while considering these, we should avoid habitual ways of thinking and employ different methods. Visualise the delicious tastes and odours of strawberries or the ever-changing odour of melon. Think about the time and energy spent in laboratories to produce similar odours and about the repeated trials that resulted in failure. Indeed, results obtained by scientists in laboratories prove to be no better than the unsuccessful imitations of their natural counterparts. The varieties of taste, odour and colour in nature bear indeed matchless attributes.

That all vegetables and fruits have distinct tastes and odours and carry individual colours is the result of the design particular to them. They are all favours Allah bestows upon man.

Similarly, animals, too, are created specially for human beings. Apart from serving as food, man finds their physical appearances ap-

pealing. Fish, corals, star-fishes decorating the depths of oceans with all their beautiful colours, all kinds of birds adding charm to their habitat or cats, dogs, dolphins and penguins... they are all favours from Allah. Allah stresses this fact in many verses:

> And He has made everything in the heavens and everything on the earth subservient to you. It is all from Him. There are certainly signs in that for people who reflect. (Surat al-Jathiyah: 13)
>
> If you tried to number Allah's blessings, you could never count them. Allah is Ever -Forgiving, Most Merciful. (Surat an-Nahl: 18)
>
> He has given you everything you have asked Him for. If you tried to number Allah's blessings, you could never count them. Man is indeed wrong-doing, ungrateful. (Surah Ibrahim: 34)

The living beings mentioned above are only a tiny part of the favours and beauties Allah bestows. Wherever we turn, we come across creations reflecting the attributes of Allah. Allah is ar-Razzaq (the Ceaseless Provider), al-Latif (the Subtle One, He who creates things most subtly), al-Karim (the Generous One), al-Barr (the source of all goodness).

Now, take a look around you and think. And never plead ignorance of the fact that everything you possess is a favour to you from your Creator:

> Any blessing you have is from Allah. Then when harm touches you, it is to Him you cry for help. (Surat an-Nahl: 53)

Never Plead Ignorance

of the Fact That You Won't Stay Long in This World

Everything that appears to be beautiful and appealing in this world decays or ages one day. The end of man is similar, and there is by no means salvation from it. From birth, man goes through a steady process of ageing, ultimately ending up in death. Everyone knows this obvious fact, yet people can't help but drift with the daily flow of events. They attach more importance to worldly tasks than they actually deserve.

However one fact renders this attachment meaningless: that life in this world has an end. It is the life in the hereafter that has no end. Chasing after benefits that one day will lose their significance is absolutely not wise. Pleading ignorance of this fact and orienting all one's efforts towards worldly objectives will lead man to an irrecoverable regret. **So, avoid this never-ending regret. Never plead ignorance of the OBVIOUS fact that your life in this world will end one day.**

People who are heavily occupied with mundane tasks and forget death ignore the supremely important fact: life in this world is rather short. Visualise the things you possess and attach importance to in this life; they will shortly decay and finally disappear. People you love will die one after another. Furniture will be broken, buildings will collapse, clothes will wear out... and everything you possess will rapidly deteriorate.

When you reflect on your past days, you realise with surprise that nothing properly satisfied you because time passed very quickly. Until this moment, it may well be that you have been unaware of this reality; yet now that you have grasped it, you must base your reasoning on more realistic grounds and reorient all your deeds and the conduct of your lives. Properly, you should try to earn the good pleasure of Allah, the Bestower of all favours in this world and the next. That is because, those who consume their lives irresponsibly will be greatly astonished in the Hereafter. When they will rise from the dead and stand before Allah, they will realise that they only stayed for a short time in this world. This fact is explained in the Qur'an in the following verse:

> He will say: "What many years did you tarry on the earth?" They will say: "We tarried there for a day or part of a day. Ask those able to count!" He will say, "You only tarried there for a little while if you did but know! (Surat al-Muminun: 112-114)

That is why you must never plead ignorance of the fact that this life is short and must never attach yourself to such short-lived values. Remember that everything is given to man to make him desire paradise and prepare for the hereafter, man's true abode.

Know that the life of this world is merely a game and a diversion and ostentation and a cause of boasting among yourselves and trying to outdo one another in wealth and children: like the plant-growth after rain which delights the cultivators, but then it withers and you see it turning yellow, and then it becomes broken stubble. In the Hereafter there is terrible punishment but also forgiveness from Allah and His good pleasure. The life of this world is nothing but the enjoyment of delusion. (Surat al-Hadid: 20)

Everything on earth is destined to perish. Everything in nature decays and reduces to insignificance in time. The most glorious places turn into ruins. Think about these facts and never plead ignorance that these images are created on purpose by Allah; to prevent you develop a profound sense of attachment to this life and forget the hereafter.

Allah created man in a most complete state and equipped him with superior characteristics. Yet, despite all its superior features, man has a rather fragile body, which is always vulnerable to external and internal threats. This creation surely serves to a purpose; to make him grasp his weakness before his Creator and to prevent him from a profound sense of attachment to this life.

Whether one is well off or poor, young or old, each moment, every human being is surrounded with similar weaknesses and imperfections.

Every man feels thirsty, hungry and tired. Moreover, he constantly needs body care to keep himself clean and fresh. Only the never-ending needs of the body pertaining to hygiene is sufficient to remind man his weaknesses. Think of a rose, for instance. It never stinks despite the fact that it grows in soil, is fed with manure, and remains in a natural environment of dust and dirt. Under all conditions, it has a delicate fragrance. We need hardly mention that it needs no body-care. However, this is not the case for man. All efforts made to keep one's body permanently clean and fresh prove to be a vain endeavour.

Disease also reminds man how prone to weakness he is. Mere viruses, invisible to the naked eye, seriously affect the body, which otherwise is highly protected against all types of external threats. Medical interventions based on the use of advanced technology and drugs still fail to contribute to the well being of human beings. Microbes penetrating through a slight cut on the skin to body may cause a detrimental consequence like death. Alternatively, a rebellious cell in the body may suddenly cause cancer. By the time one learns he is cancer, it may be too late to treat this deadly disease.

Accidents also pose serious threats to man. There are thousands of factors surrounding us that may suddenly divert the flow of our lives. One may lose his balance and fall in the middle of the street, for instance. A haemorrhage in the brain or a broken leg may well be traced back to

Everyday, accidents constitute a considerable part of radio and TV news. Remember that there is no reason why one day, your or one of your immediate family members' name, would not appear in these news.

such an ordinary accident. Or, while eating supper, one may choke to death on a fish-bone. One who ponders over these facts surely displays no futile devotion to this world. **Therefore, as a man of understanding, you never plead ignorance that your body is created inherently weak to remind you that this world is temporary. Draw lessons from these incidents and situations which serve as admonitions and warnings and put all your efforts not to lose an eternal life of bliss and ease.**

Ageing is one of the issues people avoid to think. However, it is the unavoidable end for every person. The destructive effects of the passage of years on body are irrecoverable. Whether rich or poor, beautiful or ugly, one ages in the rapid flow of time….The effects of years become obvious firstly on face. Initially wrinkles around eyes and mouth appear and the colour of the skin becomes dull. The state of the skin of hands and neck almost manifest the old age. Bones become weaker and man starts to suffer from impaired thinking. These are the unavoidable consequences of ageing and man can never stop this process, though he shuns thinking about it:

> **Allah created you and then will take you back again. And some of you revert to the lowest form of life so that after having knowledge, you know nothing at all. Allah is All-Knowing, All-Powerful. (Surat an-Nahl: 70)**

Never plead ignorance of the fact that, sooner or later, you will age one day and lose your physical strength like these people shown in the pictures.

As one grows older, physical and spiritual characteristics pertaining to childhood become more obvious. Elderly people fail to do many tasks requiring physical strength. It is possible that man could remain young until he dies. Yet Allah reminds man about the temporary nature of this world by making the quality of his life deteriorate at certain phases of life. Comprehending these facts, man avoids displaying a deep attachment to this life.

You also must never plead ignorance about the fact that one day you will also grow old and lose most of your physical and mental skills. So, while you are still endowed with these skills, start getting prepared for the hereafter.

The world is anything but serene and still. We are all vulnerable to natural threats, both internal and external. Meteor showers, asteroids are only a few of the factors likely to pose threats to the world from space. As for the solid earth, the planet's interior has an inner core of molten elements. It surely would not be an exaggeration to call this part of the earth, which remains invisible to our eyes, "a flaming core". There also exists an atmosphere surrounding the earth, which is a "shield" against external threats. Yet, no part of the earth is immune from the effects of atmospheric forces like thunderstorms, storms, or hurricanes.

Natural hazards may strike at any time. Though rarely, they cause considerable loss of life and property damage. Generally referred to as "natural disasters", earthquakes, lightning, flash floods, global wildfires, acid rain, and tidal waves have different intensities and effects. What is common to all these disasters is the fact that in just moments they can reduce a city, with all its inhabitants, to ruin. What is most important, no human being has the power to combat or prevent any of these hazards.

Despite being aware of this fact and frequently coming across with such incidents, majority of men pretend not to understand these issues. Each disaster is a reminder that developing an attachment for this life is a vain effort. These are surely warnings to those that can contemplate the significance of such events and draw lessons from them:

Do they not see that they are tried once or twice in every year? But still they do not turn back. They do not pay heed. (Surat at-Tawbah: 126).

Remember that each disaster is a reminder for human beings that the world is anything but serene and still. So, you never plead ignorance that, through these disasters, your Creator is warning you.

In the Qur'an, Allah informs us that He showed the right path to all people throughout world history and warned them through His messengers of the Day of Judgement and hell. These messengers became the leaders of faith in their separate societies and communicated the limits man has to observe to earn the good pleasure of Allah.

However, a majority of these people denounced the messengers sent to them and showed animosity towards them. The relevant verse follows:

How many cities spurned their Lord's command and His Messengers! And so We called them harshly to account and punished them with a terrible punishment. They tasted the evil consequences of what they did and the end of their affair was total loss. (Surat at-Talaq: 8-9)

As stated in the Qur'an, those communities who rejected to submit to the call of messengers faced various disasters. These disasters actually befell abruptly, at a time they never expected. However, we should consider one significant fact: those communities who resisted obeying the commands of Allah did not suffer from Allah's wrath without warnings. Allah sent them messengers to warn them with the hope that they would regret their behaviour and submit to Him. Yet, because of their arrogance, they brought Allah's wrath down upon themselves and were wiped off the face of the earth quite suddenly. The Qur'an gives an account of the stories of some communities:

And to Madyan We sent their brother Shu'ayb, he said: "My people, worship Allah and look to the Last Day and do not act unjustly on earth corrupting it." But they denied him so the earthquake seized them and morning found them lying flattened in their homes. (Surat al-'Ankabut: 36-37) We seized Pharaoh's people with years of droughts and scarcity of fruits so that hopefully they would pay heed. (Surat al-A'raf: 130)

Disasters are constant reminders of the fact that the world is full of internal and external threats. Man never assumes that he might also be affected by such a disaster one day. Yet, Allah has the power to make him face such a terrible incident at a very unexpected time.

But when We removed the plague from them –for a fixed term which they fulfilled – they broke their word. Then We took revenge on them and drowned them in the sea because they denied Our Signs and paid no attention to them. (Surat al-A'raf: 135-136)

Exulting in affluence, some societies who led an extravagant life deserved Allah's wrath. These societies actually prepared the bitter end they faced with their own hands. Yet, despite all the crimes they committed against the Will of Allah, they still assumed that the approaching disaster was good for them.

How many wrongdoing cities We destroyed, and now all their roofs and walls are fallen in; how many abandoned wells and stuccoed palaces! Have they not travelled about the earth and do they not have hearts to understand with or ears to hear with? It is not their eyes which are blind but the hearts in their breasts which are blind. (Surat al-Hajj: 45-46)

When they saw it as a storm cloud advancing on their valleys they said, "This is a storm cloud which will give us rain." No, rather it is what you desired to hasten – a wind containing painful punishment, destroying everything at its Lord's command! When morning came you could see nothing but their dwellings. That is how We repay the people of the evildoers. (Surat al-Ahqaf: 24-25)

Do not repeat the mistake of these people. Never plead ignorance of the fact that you should draw lessons from the experience of the preceding generations that did not take admonition from the warnings of Allah. As stated in the verse **"as to the Thamud, We guided them, but they preferred blindness to guidance....."** (Surah Fussilat: 17), do not prefer blindness and disregard that you should take admonition from all events your Lord makes you live through:

How many wrongdoing cities We destroyed, and now all their roofs and walls are fallen in; how many abandoned wells and stuccoed palaces! (Surat al-Hajj: 45)

Have they not travelled about the earth and do they not have hearts to understand with or ears to hear with? It is not their eyes which are blind but the hearts in their breasts which are blind. (Surat al-Hajj: 46)

Never Plead Ignorance

of the Fact that Death is Inevitable

*D*eath is an unavoidable end. Like all the other people who lived in the past, the ones who will live in the future will also die. Nobody, without exception, can escape it. That is why this is one of the issues human beings avoid thinking and talking about. Some people insistently avoid the thought that one day they will lose everything to which they are attached with desire, and they will stand before Allah to give an account of the deeds they did in this life.

Since, so far, not a single soul has escaped death, how can these people behave so heedlessly? How can they lead their lives as if they will never face death one day?

People often invent scenarios in their minds. They want to believe, for instance, that they will die in the later years of their lives and that hence they still have years ahead. Contrary to what they believe however, they hear almost everyday news of young people who lose their lives. Hearses which they see on television, or which they come across on the streets or cemeteries they pass by every day remind them of death. Yet, they pretend not to understand the fact of death.

However, death is always on the watch for man. It is possible that anyone could breathe his last in the blink of an eye. Any time, he may face angels assigned to take his soul. From then on, he loses all his chances to save himself from an everlasting grievous punishment. Nothing surely compensates for a life spent in heedlessness.

Never abandon yourself to this heedlessness, which seizes many people, and never plead ignorance of the fact that death is but a momentary transition and that it is very close to every soul.

People assume they can take precautions against death. This is however a senseless conviction. No matter where the person is, by whom he is surrounded, or under which circumstances he leads his life, it is unlikely that he could avoid death. Allah draws our attention to this fact in the following verses:

Say: "Death from which you are fleeing, will certainly catch up with you. Then you will be returned to the Knower of the Unseen and the Visible and He will inform you about what you did." (Surat al-Jumu'ah: 8)

Whereever you are, death will catch up with you, even if you are in impregnable fortresses. If a good thing happens to them, they say, "This has come from Allah." But if a bad thing happens to them, they say, "This has come from you." Say, "Everything has come from Allah." What is the matter with these people that they scarcely understand a single word? (Surat an-Nisa: 78)

Every self will taste death. We test you with both good and evil as a trial. And you will be returned to Us. (Surat al-Anbiya: 35)

Everyday we hear of the death of someone or we lose one of our close relatives. These incidents are surely OBVIOUS evidence that no one can avoid death. Whether young or old, well-off or poor, every one faces death on a predestined day. This makes one realise that one should not attach to this world and prepare for the life after death.

Never plead ignorance of the fact that a person merely deceives himself by assuming that death is far from him. And being aware of this fact, spend your life in earning the good pleasure of Allah.

Avoiding the thought of death does not change the fact that one will die one day. A sudden traffic accident or a clot on the brain may well be the unexpected end of a young and healthy person. Nobody can claim that he will not die falling down steps or on the way to a business meet-

In the course of his life, a person frequently comes upon such scenes in papers and on the TV. He, however, never thinks that one day his body will be placed in that coffin by his relatives, and carried to the graveyard. Never forget that one day they will also carry your coffin just the same way. You will stay for a short time in this world and be returned to your Lord.

ing. This being the case, it is also irrational that one thinks one can avoid death by not giving a thought to it. Nobody knows where or under which circumstances he will die. Allah may take back the soul of any one at any moment.

In the rush of daily hassles, everyday you wake to a new day. That there are a lot of things to accomplish probably makes you feel that it is too early to die. However, this is just avoidance of death and these are only vain endeavours to escape it. Death is a reality you may meet any time, and time flies in the countdown to one's own death.

Never plead ignorance of this OBVIOUS fact, and do not be seized by death in a state of heedlessness.

Disbelievers often carry strange convictions about death. This fact is stressed in the Qur'an as follows:

> **Persisting in immense wrongdoing and saying, "When we are dead and turned to dust and bones, shall we then be raised again or our forefathers, the earlier peoples?" Say: "The earlier and the later peoples will certainly all be gathered to the appointment of a specified day. (Surat al-Waqi'ah: 47-50)**

As stated in the verses above, death is not the beginning of an eternal sleep in one's grave. Death is the gate through which one passes to one's eternal abode after giving an account of one's deeds in this world. Death, which is merely the moment one leaves the body and all attachments to this life, is by no means the end of everything. On the contrary, it is the beginning of real life.

Allah, in the Qur'an, which guides humanity to the true path, repeatedly reminds us of the temporary nature of this world, of death, the existence of the life beyond and the need to prepare for it, summoning us to clarity of mind and consciousness. Likewise, all the messengers of Allah invited their peoples to the religion of truth, and only demanded of them that they reorient their hearts and their deeds for the sake of Allah. The moment of death is the beginning of a day when the deeds of all people will be reckoned. **So, never plead ignorance of the fact that death is the key to the gate of the eternal abode. Spend your life without forgetting the fact of death.** Such a thought surely leads man to the right-acting way of life that will save one from eternal punishment.

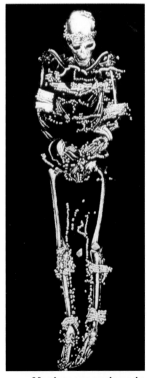

All possessions one endeavours to attain in this life – money, respect and power – are only values of this world. Despite knowing that all these values will one day slip out of their hands, people cannot help but develop deep attachment to these values. Though it is obvious that one day they will, in every case, leave these possessions in this world, they still pretend not to understand this and they endeavour to forget the fact of death.

In such a state of spirit, human beings develop an ambitious attachment to this life. Throughout history, all fir'awns and most of the prominent people in different societies assumed

Man's possessions in this world do no good to him when he turns to a heap of bones in his grave.

that their possessions would make them immune to death. Furthermore, some famous queens were buried along with innumerable treasures, but that did not save their bodies from being reduced to skeletons.

However, a person who ponders on death will realise the futility of devotion to this life and start to live for his true abode, the hereafter. **Never plead ignorance of the fact that the possessions of this life will remain behind in this world. Avoid the deep regret people will feel in the hereafter.**

Think about a man who does not ponder on death all through his life, who does not take heed from the events Allah makes him experience, who does not respond to the call of Allah's messengers and accordingly who spends his life without believing Allah. A person who follows his vain desires will surely be seized abruptly by death. Regretful, he will demand another chance to return to life. However, there will be no return.

Never plead ignorance of the fact that those who avoid the thought of death will face a fearsome end. So, before that day, rearrange all your deeds, keeping in mind that nobody guarantees you eternal life on this earth, for it is a day on which no regret will save one from eternal grief.

> **Give from what We have provided for you before death comes to one of you and he says, "My Lord, if only you would give me a little more time so that I can give in charity and be among the righteous!" Allah will not give anyone more time, once their time has come. Allah is aware of what you do. (Surat al-Munafiqun: 10-11)**
>
> **When death comes to one of them, he says: "My Lord, send me back again, so that perhaps I may act rightly regarding the things I failed to do!" No indeed! It is just words he utters. Before them there is an interspace until the day they are raised up. (Surat al-Muminun: 99-100)**
>
> **There is no repentance for people who persist in doing evil until death comes to them and who then say, "Now I repent," nor for people who die rejecting faith. We have prepared for them a painful punishment. (Surat an-Nisa: 18)**

Never Plead Ignorance

of the Fact that the Qur'an is the Just Book and that You Will Be Judged According to It

The foremost thing someone who has faith in Allah should do is to know Allah and His Messengers with true knowledge and then to know his responsibilities to Him, his sole Creator. The source which provides this knowledge to man is the Qur'an. In the Qur'an, Allah gives His commands and the limits He ordains for man. Man can attain eternal salvation only when he worships Allah alone without any partner and does his best to meticulously observe these commands and limits. In the Hereafter, the rewards of those who eagerly observe these limits and strive to attain His good pleasure and those who disregard them and try to satisfy their own desires will obviously not be the same.

Allah, in the Qur'an, gives a detailed account of the type of slave who will earn His Countenance. Hence, the primary responsibility of man is to practice what Allah commands in His Book. On the Day of Judgement, people will be judged according to their obedience to the Qur'an:

So hold fast to what has been revealed to you. You are on a right path. It is certainly a reminder to you and to your people and you will be questioned. (Surat az-Zukhruf: 43-44)

That is why you must never pretend you don't grasp that all people should answer the call of Allah and that to this end, they should be knowledgeable of the Qur'an.

The Qur'an, the unique guide providing man all answers and explanations about eternal salvation, is a reminder and an admonition. Allah relates this attribute of the Qur'an in many verses:

> **This is a communication to be transmitted to mankind so that they may be warned by it and so that they will know that He is One God and so that people of intelligence will pay heed. (Surah Ibrahim: 52)**
> **This is a clear explanation for all mankind, and guidance and admonition for those who have taqwa (awe or fear of Allah). (Surah Ali 'Imran: 138)**
> **No indeed! It is truly a reminder to which anyone who wills may pay heed. But they will only pay heed if Allah wills. He is entitled to be feared and entitled to forgive. (Surat al-Muddaththir: 54-55)**

The warnings and advice that Allah gives in the Qur'an are of great significance. A person should re-orient the conduct of his life in accordance with them. Otherwise, societies, where violent disorders and restlessness prevail, will spring up. Such a society becomes unreliable and insecure since people do not observe the limits Allah commands. That is why complying with the commands of Allah is of great importance. Those who have fear of Allah heed these warnings and pay meticulous attention to them and to putting them into practice in their daily lives. It is OBVIOUS that a life shaped according to one's own personal principles and moral values, totally ignoring the Qur'anic standpoint, will not help one attain eternal salvation.

Do not make the same mistake as many others. Never pretend you don't grasp that you do not have a guide other than the Qur'an and that the Qur'an is a reminder and an admonition.

Each verse Allah relates in the Qur'an is extremely comprehensible and explicit. Therefore when anyone says "I read the Qur'an yet I could not understand it", one should also be aware that this is just a pretext to avoid his responsibility to Allah and a misdeed for which he will be judged on the Day of Judgement. For those who sincerely turn to Allah and seek guidance, the verses of the Qur'an are comprehensible. That the commands of Allah are comprehensible means that we have the responsibility for practising them. Pretending not to grasp this OBVIOUS fact and claiming not to understand the verses is definitely an unjust stance. Allah relates in the verses that the Qur'an can be readily understood:

> **Am I to desire someone other than Allah as a judge when it is He who has sent down the Book to you clarifying everything? Those We have given the book know it has been sent down from your Lord with truth, so on no account be among the doubters. (Surat al-An'am: 114)**
>
> **In this way We have sent it down as clear signs. Allah guides anyone He wills. (Surat al-Hajj: 16)**

So, never pretend you don't grasp that all verses of the Qur'an are explicit and easy to practise. Do not follow a path you will later regret.

Allah protects the Qur'an, and it has been maintained unaltered for 1,400 years. Allah relates this fact in the following verses:

> **It is We Who have sent down the Reminder and We Who will preserve it. (Surat al-Hijr: 9)**
>
> **The Words of your Lord are perfect in truthfulness and justice. No one can change His Words. He is the All-Hearing, the All-Knowing. (Surat al-An'am: 115)**

These promises of Allah are certainly sufficient for believers. However, Allah also equipped the Qur'an with some scientific and numeric miracles, revealing once again that it is a Book from Him. Apart from the miraculous characteristic of the Qur'an, it also has a "mathematical miracle". An example of this is the numbers of repetitions of some words in the Qur'an. Some words are surprisingly repeated in numbers which relate to the meanings of the words. Below are such words and the numbers of their repetitions in the Qur'an.

- The statement of "seven heavens" is repeated seven times.
- The number of times the words, "world " and "hereafter" are repeated is also the same: 115
- "Day (yawm)" is repeated 365 times in singular form while "month" (shehr) is repeated 12 times.

• The word "faith" (iman) (without genitive) is repeated 25 times throughout the Qur'an, as is also the word "infidelity or covering over the truth" (kufr).

• When we count the word "Say", we come up with the result of 332. We see the same figure when we count the word "they said".

• The word "devil" (shaytan) is used 88 times. The word "angel" is also repeated 88 times.

These attributes of the Qur'an reveal definitely that it is a Book from Allah. So, do not pretend that you do not grasp this OBVIOUS fact.

The Qur'an is the revelation of Allah. The Qur'an, the divine guide and declaration to humankind, is a sublime Book explaining Allah's religion to all humankind. All the disbelievers' attacks on Allah's religion, seeking to raise doubts in the hearts, including the slander that "the Qur'an is a Book written by the Prophet", are all doomed. In the Qur'an, Allah challenges man to bring a book similar to the Qur'an, if they ever could:

> **Do they say, "Who has invented it?" Say: "Then produce a sura(chapter) like it and call on anyone you can besides Allah if you are telling the truth." (Surah Yunus: 38)**
>
> **Say: "If both men and jinn banded together to produce the like of this Qur'an, they could never produce anything like it, even if they backed each other up." (Surat al-Isra: 88)**

Despite all the divine attributes of the Qur'an, those disbelievers who pretend not to grasp these attributes will surely have come to a sharp understanding in the Hereafter. Yet it will be too late. **So, don't be like those who raise doubts about the authenticity of the Qur'an, and don't pretend not to understand that the Qur'an is the just book of Allah and no one can bring another book similar to it.**

Never Plead Ignorance

About The Voice of Your Conscience

During the course of life, man is tested in his reactions to the incidents he encounters and in his inner thoughts. During this trial we encounter two alternatives: we either listen to the voice of our divine guide, our conscience, or we conform to the lowest form of our selves, which initially always lead to wrong. Allah draws attention to these two voices in the following verses:

And the self and what proportioned it and inspired it with depravity or taqwa. (Surat ash-Shams: 7-8)

The unregenerate self, which is the lowest form of the human self (nafs) turns to rebellion, evil and disobedience of Allah's commands. It actually obeys evil prompting man to disregard attaining the good pleasure of Allah and to be committed to his own desires. The evil does this stealthily. If a person does not listen to the voice of his conscience, he will simply be deceived by evil whisperings of his self.

However, in every circumstance, the conscience never remains quiet until one breathes his last. Despite the stealthy inculcation of the evil, the conscience commands us to do virtuous and blessed deeds.

Surely this is a matchless system and a great favour Allah grants man. No matter which incident man encounters in life, no matter where he goes or what origin he has, he possesses a guide to the truth. **Always keep in mind that you possess a guide to the truth. Never pretend that you don't understand this inner voice.**

Furthermore, conscience is not an inspiration peculiar only to believers. It exists in every individual, including disbelievers. However, that
believers always comply with the voice of their conscience makes them
different. Disbelievers, on the other hand, satisfy their own desires despite what their consciences tell them. Allah draws attention to this subject in a story about Ibrahim. In the Qur'an, Allah relates the following di-
alog between Ibrahim and his people which occurred after Ibrahim broke
the idols, which his people worshipped, except the biggest one:

> They said, "Did you this to our gods, Ibrahim?" He said: "No, this one, the
> biggest of them, did it. Ask them if they are able to speak!" They consult-
> ed among themselves and said, "It is you yourselves who are wrongdo-
> ers." But then they relapsed back into their disbelief: "You know full well
> these idols cannot talk." (Surat al-Anbiya: 62-65)

The people who uttered these words were actually the ones who decided to cast Ibrahim to the fire. Even these people, so cruel in attempting
to kill a prophet who was assigned the duty of guiding them to the truth,
had consciences telling them the truth. Yet as the verse suggests, **"they
were blind and deaf"** (Surat al-Ma'idah: 71), they pretended not to understand the truth.

Like every other man, you have both a conscience and an evil who
misleads you. You also hear the voices of your conscience and your evil.
**If you want to attain the good pleasure of Allah and truthfulness, don't
pretend that you don't hear the voice of your conscience.**

A person may feel concerned that he is not able to distinguish these
two voices. Yet, keep in mind that conscience does not fail to see the truth
for a moment; it instantly tells the truth. However, as one hears this voice,
the evil immediately tries to mislead the self. The self makes various excuses. The evil strives to thwart one from doing what one's conscience
whispers. In other words, encountering an incident, what one initially
hears is the voice of the conscience. All the excuses we make against following this voice are the voice of one's self. **At the moment you hear this
voice of the conscience, don't pretend you don't grasp that this voice,**

calling you to the good pleasure of Allah, is your conscience.

If one ignores the voice of the conscience, in time, one becomes almost a slave of the self, becoming prone to any kind of wickedness. Since such an attitude is merely an expression of one's own preference, one fails this test, and loses the blessed eternal life, whose loss is eternal deprivation. Man bears the sole responsibility of being a slave of Allah, which can only be achieved by acting by the Book and by following one's conscience. Allah calls the end of those who pretend not to understand this fact 'failure' in the following verse:

> **He who purifies it has succeeded, he who covers it up has failed. (Surat ash-Shams: 7-8)**

Surely almost every one has experienced the inner pain that regret gives. The main cause of this feeling is not following the commands of conscience, which is also a divine warning to man. In some circumstances, this pain is not relieved until one amends one's misdeeds or changes one's flawed preferences; it simply turns into spiritual torture. **So, do not pretend you don't grasp it, when you are full of remorse.** This is surely a sign of a misdeed you have done; your conscience has already told you what you did wrong and where you did it. Take this chance to compensate for your misdeeds in this world, while there is still a chance. In the Hereafter, the regret you will feel will be unbearable and will remain with you for all eternity, unless it is for the forgiveness of Allah and His mercy.

Even though your self thinks of it as a difficult task or it is unwilling to follow the conscience, don't pretend that you don't grasp your conscience is guiding you to the truth. Be certain that Allah has infinite conscience; if you persist in following the Qur'an and are alert to what your conscience commands, then Allah will bountifully reward you for all your deeds, even for the ones that may seem insignificant to you. Meanwhile, surely those who remain heedless of the Book and about their consciences will not be treated the same in the presence of Allah.

Never Plead Ignorance

of the Fact that Allah Commands Man to Conduct Himself Correctly

*T*he nature of man is inherently inclined to practise the values of character praised in the Book. Allah revealed the Qur'an, the unique source explaining the values most conforming with the natural inclination of mankind. A man attains true bliss, satisfaction and peace only when he displays complete obedience to the commands of Allah, openly as well as secretly, with wholesome eagerness. Allah relates this in the following verse:

> So set your face firmly towards the religion, as a pure natural believer, Allah's natural believer, Allah's natural pattern on which He made mankind. There is no changing Allah's creation. That is the true religion – but most people do not know it – turning towards him. (Surat ar-Rum: 30)

Those who do not observe the limits set by Allah and ignore the Qur'anic values incur unthinkable trouble in their lifetime. That is simply because, in a society where the bounties of Allah are abused, the criteria upon which one determines the right and wrong alter from one person to another. Hence, millions of different criteria ceaselessly clash with each other. By statements starting with "In my opinion…", every individual endeavours to impose his own convictions on others. He orients the conduct of his daily life to gaining personal interests. However, in the Qur'an, man is summoned to a single truth, to the path of Allah.

> It is not devoutness to turn your faces to the East or to the West. Rather

those with true devoutness are those who believe in Allah and the Last Day, the Angels, the Book, and the Prophets, and who, despite their love for it give away their wealth to their relatives, and to orphans and the very poor, and to travellers and beggars and to set slaves free, and who establish salat (the prayer) and pay zakat (regular charity); those who honour their contracts when they make them, and are stedfast in poverty and in illness and in battle. Those are the people who are true. They are the people who have taqwa. (Surat al-Baqarah: 177)

Adherence to the Qur'an in an effort to seek Allah's Countenance and to attain His good pleasure, makes a believer always pursue perfection in manners. Such a person always seeks the good for others and does it for no price at all. Furthermore, he does not do it to be appreciated. In compliance with the command of Allah, he reacts to bad behaviour with excellent character. He has fear of Allah, and all his attitudes, decisions and reactions reflect this fear. That is why, at any moment, he demonstrates exemplary virtuous conduct as much as he is able.

Nevertheless, there exists no mechanism or reason preventing a man from engaging in misdeeds who does not fear Allah and who believes that when death befalls him – even if in a few decades – he will cease to exist for all eternity. It is not reasonable to expect such a person to be patient, generous or to remain loyal to somebody else for no price. Such a person simply has no reason to display excellent character, except for the cowardly thought that if he doesn't harm others perhaps they won't harm him and if he shows good conduct to them perhaps they will show it to him. On the contrary, he believes such virtuous conduct to be idiotic and a mere loss, except in the selfish form we note. That is because, he believes he will not be rewarded in return for his good deeds in this world and he has no faith in the Hereafter. In this respect, he overcomes every obstacle to attain his selfish goals. Man is prone to abstain from things likely to harm him. Especially, if he believes he will receive punishment in return for bad behaviour, he will never dare to do it. Yet, people who are distant from religion do not refrain from such behaviour, except from shortsighted self-interest.

So, don't pretend you don't grasp that the true values can only be displayed when people observe the limits of Allah. Otherwise, degeneration prevails. If you also want to lead a beautiful life in this world, keep in mind that you have to turn to the religion of Allah.

The sincerity and honesty of a person are the basic indications of the character values with which he strives to earn the good pleasure of Allah. Man is responsible to nobody else but Allah. It is only Allah who will judge man on the Day of Judgement. Therefore, it is not sensible to resort to lies and insincere behaviour under the guidance of selfish interests and motives. **So, don't plead ignorance of the fact that you have no alternative but to be sincere and honest in your conduct while Allah surrounds you and hears and sees whatever you do.**

Another indication of good character is modesty. Arrogance and modesty can never remain together. It is obvious that an arrogant person can neither nurture love and mercy in his heart for others nor be generous. A person, however, should be aware of the fact that he personally possesses nothing of which to be proud. If his arrogance is due to his possessions, then he should know that the heavens, the earth and everything in between belong solely to Allah. Allah grants intelligence, good looks and skills to man and it is only a matter of a moment for Him to take them back. Furthermore, man is mortal. He will go alone into the presence of Allah, leaving everything granted him behind. Allah also states in the Qur'an that those who are arrogant in this world will be humbled before Him.

This is surely the truth. Man has nothing to take pride in. No matter how wealthy, beautiful, famous or respected you are, don't pretend you don't grasp this fact! What will make a man fortunate is the good character with which he strives to attain the good pleasure of Allah, and his submission to Him.

Allah gives a detailed account of virtuous, blessed behaviour and attitudes in the Qur'an. Below, the typical attributes of an individual who is sincerely devoted to Allah and who is aware that he will be judged can be listed as follows:

Reliability,

Forgiveness,

Repelling evil with good,

Having mercy for believers,

Not being led astray by rage,

Engaging in good deeds for no price or reward,

Remaining consistently temperate in one's approach to people

Avoiding ridiculing people because of jealousy and selfishness,

Speaking graciously to people,

Keeping promises and trusts,

Being a reliable witness,

Avoiding vain talk and trifling,

Being generous,

Settling matters wisely

Being patient,

Being modest...

The attributes of believers listed above are only the basic ones. On the Day of Judgement, man will be judged according to what actions he has done and these attributes. Those who have these attributes in this world and who have acted according to the Book, on the other hand, will be rewarded with a beautiful life:

> When those who have taqwa of Allah are asked, "What has your Lord sent down?" their reply is, "Good!" There is good in the world for those who do good, and the abode of the Hereafter is even better. How wonderful is the abode of those who have taqwa: Gardens of Eden which they enter, with rivers flowing under them, where they have whatever they desire. That is how Allah repays those who have taqwa. (Surat an-Nahl: 30-31)
>
> Not so! All who submit themselves completely to Allah and are good-doers will find their reward with their Lord. They will feel no fear and will know no sorrow. (Surat al- Baqarah: 112)

No matter under which circumstances you are, it is essential for your eternal life that you never plead ignorance of the fact that you have to live up to the values of the Qur'an.

Never Plead Ignorance

of the Fact that Disbelief is the Source of All Wickedness

A man having faith in the existence of Allah proceeds on His path all through his life. He meticulously obeys His commands and spends his life in the way of Allah. For this end, a believer adopts Islam, the religion Allah perfected for man, and adheres to the Qur'an as a guide to the true path, taking the high manners of our prophet recounted in the Qur'an as an example for himself. Trying to follow the noble examples related in the Qur'an, his conscience leads him to strive with good character at every moment of his life. This is the conscience of a man who fears Allah, being aware that Allah creates life, death and the hereafter just as He creates man.

Those who insist on denying the existence of Allah, or who simply reject surrendering themselves to Allah and practising His religion fail to attain the standard of the religion of Allah since they never grasp the beauties and good aspects of the values encouraged by the Qur'an. That is why a community of disbelievers consists of people who live properly and decently not for the good pleasure of Allah but for the approval of other people, and others who dare to live immorally without considering its consequences.

Telling lies, taking bribes, murder, suicide, gambling, violating the rights of others or committing injustices are the misdeeds readily committed by people having no fear of Allah. They do them either openly or by legal subterfuges. They cannot keep their rage under control, are inherently jealous and ambitious and easily hurt others by the way they speak. They are not self-sacrificing and are dominated by selfish desires and petty interests. There may be some people saying "I am not religious yet I do not have hatred for people either." Yet, it is probable that one day such people will encounter an incident that will enrage them. At such a moment, they may well engage in any kind of wickedness that they would normally never dare. After killing somebody, for instance, it is most probable that they would say, "but he deserved it." This is a consequence one would never expect from someone who feels fear for Allah. That is because a person who has faith in Allah is known for his patience and that he would never dare to do something Allah prohibits. Hence, he would never knowingly give in to his anger.

It is, on the other hand, possible that a disbeliever would say, " I have no faith yet I would never take a bribe." However such a statement remains only a claim since he is able to do any misdeed when he feels under pressure. People often try to find legitimate pretexts to justify a bribe saying, for instance, that they need money to get the kids through school. Yet, it is unlikely that you would expect such an approach from a believer. A person having fear of Allah never engages in deeds he knows will be judged severely on the Day of Judgement.

Some common crimes provide good examples of such insincere attitudes. Theft, for instance, as an established offence, may well be regarded as legitimate by these people under certain circumstances. Towels, glasses, cutlery taken from hotels are not considered theft by this mentality. When viewed from the point of the religion, however, under all circumstances theft is immoral.

All these are actually the common attributes of people who do not have fear of Allah. Hundreds of examples can be given to depict this character. Never showing commitment to attain excellent character, these people make a sacrifice only when they feel they have a serious interest in it. As soon as they find this interest to be at stake, however, they cease to make sacrifices. A believer however has a strong determination. The fear of Allah ensures this determination. This fear is also the warranty of the security religion provides for the society.

Love, mercy, respect, loyalty together with other values the family ensures also disappear in such a society. The only ones who show mercy and loyalty without price are the believers who fear Allah and believe in their individual accountability for actions.

A family laying its foundations on mercy, love and sacrifice together with the other values the Qur'an brings is essential to the welfare and peace of a society. In societies where life is not regulated by revealed values, the society degenerates, since the family, a key unit of the society, degenerates.

Only fear of Allah and faith secure peaceful societies and they are the simple consequences of adherence to the Qur'an as a life-guide. These are OBVIOUS facts.

In societies where disbelief prevails, social anarchy reigns. The wealthy oppress the poor, the poor feel hatred for the wealthy, bosses assume an aggressive attitude towards employees and vice-versa. Instead of mercy, those who are in need are shown anger.

News items of murder or suicide frequently appearing in the press have only one reason: disbelief. Surely a person killing a man only because he feels hatred for him or he derives a benefit from his death does not think that he will be judged for it. These offences readily committed by people having no fear of Allah are the type of behaviours disturbing the order and peace of society.

In such a society one does not expect to find concepts like co-operation or generosity. People do not care for each other. Similarly, the health and well-being of others never become a matter of concern. Precautions are not taken to remove anything likely to give harm to people and the society as a whole. Nobody cares about somebody becoming sick and fainting in the middle of the street, for instance. Such a person is left all alone to handle such a serious problem. Trying to derive maximum benefits, they do not hesitate to defraud each other. A market owner sells rotten food without considering the health risks to which it exposes public. Alternatively, sellers overcharge their customers. There is no end to these examples. In such a system all services rendered are bound to the price paid for them. A doctor shows the care due to his patient only when he thinks he will be well paid. In brief, the majority of these people bear sacrifices only when a solid benefit is assured.

As we have seen, there is no end to social problems and immoral attitudes where disbelief rages. **So, never plead ignorance of the fact that you need to submit yourself to the religion of Allah and that only then can you attain peace and security. Besides that, keep in mind that only a life devoted to Allah will secure a life for all eternity.**

Immorality, a consequence of disbelief, is primarily a detriment to health and the main source of trouble for the heart. A person, for instance, who makes the life of others unbearable due to his jealousy in fact lives a life that is troublesome to himself. The rage he feels is the main cause of his trouble. Mostly, other people do not realise the feelings jealous people harbour or simply do not care about them. After all, the jealousy others feel does not affect them. Consequently jealousy only negatively affects the person himself. Allah draws our attention to the trouble disbelievers suffer in the following verse:

When Allah desires to guide someone, He expands his breast to Islam. When He desires to misguide someone, He makes his breast narrow and constricted as if he were climbing up into the sky. That is how Allah defiles those who do not believe. (Surat Al-An'am: 125)

People of the religion feel pleased at the good deeds of other believers. They derive pleasure from one another's good qualities. The beauty of a person reminds a believer of the power of creation of Allah. It is also a way in which he glorifies Allah. In an environment where disbelief dominates, however, the way people hurt each other – gossiping or giving contemptuous nicknames to people – creates tension. This tension is surely a consequence of their jealousy of each other. Therefore, those who behave immorally suffer great trouble themselves for the impatient, unbalanced qualities of character they display. In other words, these people give torment to themselves. In a verse Allah says:

Allah does not wrong people in any way; rather it is people who wrong themselves. (Surah Yunus: 44)

A person having fear for Allah often shows patience no matter what he encounters in life. Difficulties neither demoralise nor discourage him. Trusting Allah, he confronts every incident with determination and courage. By trusting Allah and with the state of spirit the religion grants man, he assesses incidents wisely. Disbelievers, however, always incur trouble and superstitious fears leading them to a hellish life. Neither societies nor individuals attain a condition of heart that finds the satisfaction the verse which follows indicates: "**... Only in the remembrance of Allah can the heart find peace.**" (Surat al-Ra'd: 28)

So, ponder on the fact that disbelief eradicates all human and beautiful feelings and never plead ignorance of the fact that those who do not submit themselves to the will of Allah live in trouble and regret both in this world and beyond.

Never Plead Ignorance

About the Existence of the Hereafter and the Day of Judgement

*T*here are various types of people on earth. Some people are honest while others are liars. Some people fear Allah and observe His limits while others revolt against Him. Surely the ends of each group will match their attitudes. Out of His infinite mercy, Allah will reward each type of people justly. This absolute promise is proclaimed in the following verse:

> Or do those who perpetrate evil deeds suppose that We will make them like those who believe and do right actions, so that their lives and deaths will be the same? How bad their judgement is! Allah created the heavens and earth with truth so that every self might be repaid for what it earned and they will not be wronged. (Surat al-Jathiyah: 21-22)

The hereafter is the place where people will be rewarded justly. This is an OBVIOUS fact. Allah is aware of every incident and knows every deed, good or wicked. **So, never plead ignorance about the existence of the Hereafter, the place where Allah's attribute of justice will be fully manifested and each deed will be rewarded justly.** Besides, keep in mind that showing indifference to this fact, and simply saying "we shall be reduced to earth when we die", will not hinder the resurrection of man and the fact that he will be judged.

It is probable that a person may well deceive himself in this world. Avoiding grasping the fact of the hereafter, he may endeavour to "make the most of it." He may well silence the voice of his conscience. Yet, this will by no means prevent his death, which is on a predestined day in the presence of Allah, and his rising from the dead, which is also predestined. Whether he grasps it or not, every individual will definitely rise from the dead to stand before Allah; that day every person will be rewarded by Allah according to his good or evil deeds. Then, he will be sent to his true abode to receive his rewards. That day, those failing to see this obvious fact as well as those who simply try to be satisfied with this world will be sent to the hell, unless Allah forgives them out of His infinite mercy. These people who deserve to be in hell since they lack even an atom's weight of true faith and have no conscience will remain there for ages.

Allah describes the thoughts, words and states of the disbelievers who pretend not to understand the existence of the hereafter, and who deny the rising from the dead in the following verse:

> Whoever Allah guides is truly guided. But as for those He leads astray, you will not find any protectors for them apart from Him. We will gather them on the Day of Rising, flat on their faces, blind, dumb and deaf. Their shelter will be Hell. Whenever the Blaze dies down, We will increase it for them. That is their repayment for rejecting Our Signs and saying, "What, when we are bones and crumbled dust, will we then be raised up as a new creation?" (Surat al-Isra: 97-98)

The answer to the question asked in the above verse is OBVIOUS: the universe in which we live abounds with evidences of the glorious creation of Allah. Surely the One who miraculously creates everything surrounding us has the strength to create their counterparts in the hereafter at any moment. Allah, in the Qur'an, addresses people who pretend not to grasp the fact of hereafter by asking questions which have clear answers:

> Do they not see that Allah, Who created the heavens and earth, has the power to create the like of them, and has appointed fixed terms for them of which there is no doubt? But the wrongdoers still spurn anything but disbelief. (Surat al-Isra: 99)

Never plead ignorance of the fact that man will be judged and accordingly rewarded for all his deeds in the hereafter, the place where

Allah's attribute of justice will be fully manifest.

The majority of people proclaim that they believe in the hereafter yet they fail to ponder on it deeply. They simply plead ignorance of the fact that there they will face everything they did in this world. They deceive themselves interpreting the hereafter, the Day of Judgement, the paradise and the hell in their own way rather than in the way that Allah introduces them in the Qur'an.

Allah gives a detailed account of the hereafter, the moment of judgement, the ones who deserve to attain the paradise as well as those who will be sent to hell. On the day Day of Judgement, every person will stand alone before Allah and give an account of all the moments he spent in the worldly life. Those who endeavoured to earn the good pleasure of Allah throughout their lives will attain the paradise and remain there for all eternity, surrounded by the bounteous favours of Allah. Those, on the other hand, who lived only for this world without considering the hereafter will face an everlasting torment, unless Allah pardons them from His mercy.

Those stating "Allah will forgive me under any circumstances", those claiming "I do no harm to others" and hence thinking that they will attain the paradise, those assuming that only observing some particular act of worship will save them from punishment, deceive themselves although they know the facts. Allah, in the Qur'an draws our attention to this reality, the reality that man is aware of the facts despite making excuses:

> **That Day the only resting place will be your Lord. That Day man will be told what he did and failed to do. In fact, man will be clear proof against himself in spite of any excuses he might offer. (Surat al-Qiyamah: 12-15)**

As Allah states in the verse above, man is a witness against himself. Each person is aware of the truth. Therefore, it is nonsensical to plead ignorance of the facts by making excuses. That there are many other ill-mannered people around is not an excuse that will save one on the Day of Judgement. Neither will the fact that one's parents and grandparents are religious people, nor feeding the poor, nor saying "I am a Muslim" yet failing to engage in good deeds to earn the good pleasure of Allah, will save one from the greatest grief, unless it be by the mercy of Allah. No matter what others do, every living soul is responsible for his own deeds. We will all stand alone before Allah and be judged alone. People make many excuses to deceive themselves: that they are very busy people, they have to earn their livelihoods to look after their children, they have professions dedicated to the improvement of mankind or what they do is more important than those other things done to attain the pleasure of Allah. Yet, it is important to remember that all these statements reflect one's own point of view – not the Qur'anic standpoint – and by no means ensure salvation from a disastrous end. Certainly, the Qur'an provides the most accurate information regarding how a man should spend his life to attain the paradise.

Those embracing ways of life other than that which is seen as good by the Qur'an, those who lose time waiting for the latter years of life to worship Allah, those who deceive themselves as well as other people by making excuses, should all keep in mind that their pretexts will not save them in the hereafter. Allah will not accept lies. Moreover, these people will not be allowed to talk on the Day of Judgement. On that day, those people who ignore the facts, abuse the bounties of Allah and do not obey the commands of Allah will express their sincere regret thus:

> **And that Day Hell is produced, that Day man will remember; but how will the remembrance help him? He will say, "Oh! If only I had prepared in advance for this life of mine!" That Day no one will punish as He punishes and no one will shackle as He shackles. (Surat al-Fajr: 23-26)**

The scenes that will take place on that day are the ultimate manifestation of the eternal justice of Allah. On that day, those following the voices of their consciences and those who do not will be distinguished from each other. **So, to avoid such regret, prepare for the hereafter and never forget that you will encounter your efforts there. Never plead that you do not grasp these facts. Do not waste your life in vain and meaningless efforts.**

This fleeting life is incomparably worthless next to the hereafter. Stately mansions, ostentatious houses surrounded by gardens, power-boats, yachts, brand new cars, night-clubs, luxury hotels, honourable professions, healthy children, beautiful and esteemed spouses...such favours granted man in this life have certainly an allure. A life may be devoted to getting possession of them. Nevertheless, even if one possessed all of them or a few of them, he would still reach the hereafter on that predestined day, leaving behind everything he had been granted.

Maybe you are also one of those who has devoted his life to possessing these favours. **However, never plead that you did not understand these favours will not save you in the Hereafter.**

At the moment when the angels assigned to take your spirits will meet you, you will depart from this world, leaving behind all your possessions. There will be no turning back and you will have no chance to see them again. Once you are resurrected, you will be judged in a totally different place, in the presence of Allah. Keep in mind that, at that moment, you will not be questioned neither about the quantity of your possessions, nor your children, nor your status, nor your education. On that predestined day, neither the most prominent statesmen, nor queens and kings that have ever lived throughout history will have superiority over other people. No close friend will search for his friend. Furthermore, disbelievers will offer their worldly goods as a ransom for their own salvation:

> **No good friend will ask about his friend even though they can see each other. An evildoer will wish he could ransom himself from the punishment of that Day, by means of his sons, or his wife or his brother, or his family who sheltered him, or everyone else on earth, if that only meant that he could save himself. But no! It is a Raging Blaze, Stripping away the limbs and scalp, which calls for all who drew back and turned away, and amassed and hoarded up. (Surat al-Ma'arij: 10-18)**

So, ponder these facts related in the verse and never plead ignorance of the fact that the grief of that day will be great, so great that anyone will try to rescue himself by offering all he has in this world as ransom.

In the following verse, Allah relates that disbelievers would like to give all that is in the world – if they ever had – just to avoid the torment in hell:

If those who did wrong owned everything on earth, and the same again with it, they would offer it as a ransom to save themselves from the evil of the punishment on the Day of Rising. What confronts them from Allah will be something they did not reckon with. (Surat az-Zumar: 47)

In fact, just a brief reflection would bring any man with a sound mind to the evident conclusion. Nobody, for instance, would decline a proposal offering an immediate life in paradise provided that they give whatever they possess in this world. Without a moment's hesitation, everybody would leave his possessions, sons, and status behind and would try to attain the paradise. This is, in fact, the sole responsibility of man: offering his possessions and self to Allah, not being seized by unnecessary ambitions in this life, living for the good pleasure of Allah and in return attaining the paradise. Yet something deceives man. The short span of his life in this world is perceived as a long one. That is why people unwisely prefer this life, which is rather short and temporary, to an eternal paradise.

On one hand, a fleeting life limited to six or seven decades and, on the other, a life that will last for all eternity.

On one hand, an endless, unprecedented and beautiful life where everything desired will be there without any effort at all, on the other hand, a short, temporary life where everything is doomed to be imperfect. No matter how young and beautiful you are, this is a life you are eventually destined to lose in a few decades or tomorrow. A life which is surely an inappropriate arena in which to satisfy any desires.

So, never ignore this fact. While you still have the opportunity to attain the matchless favours of the paradise, never silence the voice of your conscience just to have the imperfect and temporary possessions of this world. Never plead ignorance about what people lose in eternity for the sake of a short life just because they do not think.

One of the main reasons why people ignore the existence of the hereafter is the fact that the majority of the people adopt such a standpoint. However this is, no doubt, the secret of the test. This is the way Allah puts people to the test. That is why Allah warns his servants against following the majority:

If you obeyed most of those on earth, they would misguide you from Allah's Way. They follow nothing but conjecture. They are only guessing. (Surat al-An'am: 116)

That the majority of people do not follow the path of Allah should by no means affect you negatively since everyone is responsible for himself. Allah, in the Qur'an, proclaims that the majority of people will not believe. It is also stated, on the other hand, that those believing will not believe without ascribing partners to Allah. One concludes from this statement the following: the majority of people do not prepare for the hereafter and that is why they will not attain the paradise. Such a state is surely not a pretext for conscientious people but a reason to feel more fear of Allah. **That is why you must never plead ignorance thinking that, "the majority of people are doing the same." Even if you are left all alone in your efforts, start to prepare for the hereafter, being aware that you are responsible only for yourself.**

Allah, in the Qur'an, describes to us the kind of effort one has to undertake for eternal salvation. On the Day of Judgement, people will be judged by their devotion to Allah, their fear of Him and the conduct this fear brings. Only a sincere devotion to Allah will secure the salvation of man in the hereafter. Allah states that neither possessions nor sons are ways to feel closer to Allah and only those who believe and engage in good deeds will attain the paradise:

It is not wealth or your children that will bring you near to Us – only in the case of people who believe and act rightly; such people will have a double recompense for what they did. They will be safe from all harm in the High Halls of Paradise. (Surah Saba: 37)

Allah relates that only taqwa, the "Fear of Allah", is worthy in His presence:

> Mankind! We created you from a male and female, and made you into peoples and tribes so that you might come to know each other. The noblest among you in Allah's sight is the one with the most taqwa. Allah is All-Knowing, All-Aware. (Surat al-Hujurat: 13)

For this reason, never plead ignorance that what will bring you eternal salvation is taqwa, and that sons, possessions and the lure of this world will be worthless in the presence of Allah.

> That abode of the Hereafter – We grant it to those who do not seek to exalt themselves in the earth or to cause corruption in it. The successful outcome is for those who have taqwa. (Surat al-Qasas: 83)

Never Plead Ignorance

of the Fact that the Hell is a Place of Torment for All Eternity

*T*he majority of people avoid thinking about the hell although they are aware of the existence of the hereafter. Pondering the bitter grief of the hell surely ensures a life devoted to Allah. This in turn urges one to reorient all one's deeds and the conduct of one's life in submission to the will of Allah. Otherwise, one will feel profound remorse. In the attempt to liberate themselves from this remorse, people ignore the existence of the hell. They attempt to alleviate the seriousness of the matter by statements like, " I don't think one would remain in hell for all eternity" or "I do not believe that Allah would punish His servants so severely." These are surely lies. Furthermore, they attempt to base these lies on the mercy of Allah. The fact is that, these people only plead ignorance about it.

Hell is the place where Allah's attribute of justice is fully manifest. Surely the rewards of those who live to earn the good pleasure of Allah all through their lives will not be the same as of those who obey evil and revolt against Allah. Allah will reward His true servants with the paradise where they will remain for all eternity. On the other hand, disbelievers will be punished in hell, a place of unbearable torment.

Allah is surely compassionate; yet pondering only His mercy and forgiveness would make one fail to recognise His other attributes. One should also be cognisant of the Creator's other attributes: Allah takes revenge from His rebellious servants and He punishes. The hell is the place where Allah will manifest these two attributes. In other words, even if people endeavour to forget, the reality of the hell is always there to encompass all disbelievers and those who seek another way than the way of Allah.

So never plead ignorance about the existence of the hereafter. Endeavouring not to think about it, or ignoring it, will not save anyone from the grievous punishment. On the contrary, people who ignore this fact and hence follow their own desires will remain in hell for all eternity, if Allah wills. The hell will be **"the meeting place"** of all these people. (Surat al-Hijr: 43)

Allah created the paradise, embellished with His favours, for His true servants who make serious efforts to attain His good pleasure throughout their lives. Allah relates the beauty of the paradise in many verses:

> **Platters and cups of gold will be passed around among them and they will have there all that their hearts desire and their eyes find delight in. You will remain in it timelessly, for ever. (Surat az-Zukhruf: 71)**

The beauty and glory of the paradise are beyond one's imagination. The Qur'anic words describing all kinds of delights (Surat ar-Rahman: 48) surely illustrate a vivid picture of the real nature of the paradise. There exist great possessions for the believers. The paradise is the place specially prepared for the believers by Allah. In it there are beautiful mansions, thrones embellished with precious stones, clothes fashioned from beads of silver, gold and pearls, rivers of honey, and never-ending fruits. They are all given to the service of believers in the paradise. The paradise is an eternal reward for believers and a manifestation of Allah's power of creation. **So, never plead ignorance of the fact that the paradise abounds with glorious favours that are incomparable with their counterparts in this life.**

Surely, there is another place manifesting Allah's matchless power of creation. The hell, created for the disbelievers, is surely another manifestation of Allah's justice. The hell is specifically created for people who disregard the fact of the hereafter, live for this world, and rebel against Allah. Just as how the paradise is adorned with remarkable favours, the hell will likewise be equipped with various types of torment.

Disbelievers will be punished for all the immoral conduct in which they engaged in this life. The punishment will surely reflect the glory of Allah. In hell, people will be subject to severe torture at every moment. With skin rent, flesh burned, the only drink of the people of hell will be blood and pus. Their shirts will be made of fire. Likewise, they will lie on beds of fire. In brief, every moment in hell will be full of anguish.

Allah, in the Qur'an, gives a detailed account of the torture disbelievers will undergo in the Hell. Disregarding this fact is by no means a way to escape. On the contrary, being aware of this fact and accordingly, feeling fear for Allah is the only way to eternal salvation of mankind.

Another subject many people ignore about the hell is the fact that the torment in hell will last for all eternity. Allah describes this fact in the Qur'an as follows:

They say: "The Fire will only touch us for a number of days." Say, "Have you made a contract with Allah – then Allah will not break His contract – or are you rather saying about Allah what you do not know?" No indeed! Those who accumulate bad actions and are surrounded by their mistakes, such people are the Companions of the Fire, remaining in it timelessly, for ever; whereas those who believe and do right actions, such people are the Companions of the Garden, remaining in it timelessly, for ever. (Surat al-Baqarah: 80-82)

As the verses suggest, punishment in the hell for relentless disbelievers is eternal. The people of paradise will remain there for all eternity. Allah relates in the following verse:

Hell lies in wait - a homecoming for the profligate remaining in it for countless aeons. (Surat an-Naba: 21-23)

Allah's decree about this subject is certain. That is why you must never plead ignorance that as long as you do not adhere to the Qur'an, there will be no salvation from hell. Those who revolt against Allah, and hence deserve the hell will remain there for all eternity.

The way a person conducts himself during the course of his short life will lead him to the place he will stay for all eternity. Surely, this is an important consequence. Accepting to be punished in the hell for all eternity just because of a life limited to 60-70 years is an OBVIOUS disaster. This OBVIOUS disaster is definitely known by every individual. However, what people fail to comprehend is the concept of "eternity."

The word "eternity" expresses a period of time that will never end. Disbelievers will always remain there: they will be subject to torture for ten years, thousands of years, billions of years, trillions of years. Trillions of years are surely insignificant next to eternity. Allah expresses this period of time in the verse above, saying, **"remaining in it for countless aeons."** (Surat an-Naba: 23)

Therefore we should not compare the trouble we undergo in this world with the eternal torment to be suffered in the hell. The severest pain in this world is limited to only six or seven decades. Even the most serious diseases have a cure, yet, the torment in the hell will never end. Therefore, never plead ignorance of what the concept "eternal" means. Compare the brevity of this life with such an endless period of life. Try to comprehend a period of time that will never end.

When you have the opportunity to remain in paradise for all eternity, avoid being punished eternally in hell, a place of total burning and destruction.

Warning!

The chapter you are about to read reveals a CRUCIAL secret of your life. You should read it very attentively and thoroughly for it concerns a subject that is liable to make a fundamental change in your outlook on the external world. The subject of this chapter is not just a point of view, a different approach, or a traditional philosophical thought: it is a fact which everyone, believing or unbelieving, must admit and which is also proven by science today. NEVER PLEAD IGNORANCE of this OBVIOUS fact.

Never Plead Ignorance

of the Fact that Matter is Only an Image

From the moment a person comes into existence, he becomes subject to the steady indoctrination of the society. A part of this indoctrination, possibly the foremost of it, holds that reality is all that can be touched with the hand and seen with the eye. This understanding, which is quite influential in society, is carried unquestioned from one generation to another.

A moment of thought, without being subject to any indoctrination, would however make one realise an astonishing fact:

From the moment we come into existence, all the things surrounding us are simply what our senses present to us. The world, human beings, animals, flowers, the colours of these flowers, odours, fruits, tastes of fruits, planets, stars, mountains, stones, buildings, space, in brief all things are perceptions our senses present us. To further clarify this subject, it will be helpful to talk about the senses, the agents providing information about the exterior world to us.

Our perceptions of seeing, hearing, smell, taste and touch, all function similarly to each other. Images we receive from objects we assume have existence in the external world (taste, odour, sound, sight, solidity) are all transmitted by neurons to the relevant centres in the brain. Hence, what the brain receives are only electrical signals. For instance, during the process of seeing, light clusters (photons) that travel from the object to the eye pass through the lens in front of the eye where they are refracted and

fall inverted on the retina at the back of the eye. The electrical signal gen-
erated by the retina is perceived as an image in the visual centre of the
brain after a series of processes. And we, in a part of our brain called the
visual centre, which takes up only a few cubic centimetres, perceive a
colourful, bright world that has depth, height and width.

A similar system applies in all the other senses. Tastes, for instance,
are turned into electrical signals by some special cells in the mouth and on
the tongue and transmitted to the relevant centre in the brain.

An example will further clarify this subject. Let's assume that at the
moment you are drinking a glass of lemonade. The coolness and solidity
of the glass you hold is converted into electrical signals by special cells
under your skin and transmitted to the brain. Simultaneously, the odour
of the lemonade, the sweet taste you experience when you sip it and the
yellow colour you see when you look at the glass are all transmitted to the
brain in the form of electrical signals. The noise you hear when you put
the glass on the table is similarly perceived by your ear and transmitted
to the brain as an electrical signal. Sensory centres in the brain that are es-
sentially different yet work in co-operation with each other interpret all of
these perceptions. As a result of this interpretation, you assume yourself

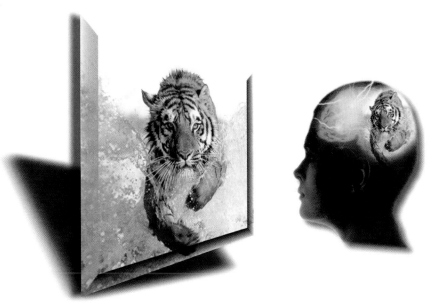

**Something you claim that you see is in fact only a perception in your brain. The world
in which you claim you are living is also nothing but a collection of perceptions.**

to drink a glass of lemonade. In other words, everything takes place in the sensory centres in the brain while you think that these perceptions have a solid existence.

However, at this point you are simply deceived since you have no evidence to assume that what you perceive in your brain has a material correlate outside your skull.

The subject that has been explained so far is an OBVIOUS fact proved true by science today. Any scientist would tell you the way this system works and that the world we live in is in reality an aggregate of perceptions. An English physicist, John Gribbin states with relation to the interpretations the brain makes that our senses are like the interpretation of stimulations coming from the external world, as if there is a tree in the garden. He goes on to say that our brain perceives the stimulations that are filtered through our senses, and that the tree is only a stimulation. He then asks: so, which one is real? The tree that is formed by our senses, or the tree in the garden?[16]

No doubt, this is a reality that requires profound reflection. Up until now, it is entirely possible you assumed that everything you see in the outer world has an absolute reality. However, as science also verifies, there is no way to prove that objects have material correlates in the outer world. The subject briefly explained here is **one of the biggest facts you can come to realize in your life; so, you never plead ignorance of this OBVIOUS fact. And start reflecting on this subject.**

So far we talked about the fact that we live in our skulls and perceive nothing more than that which our senses perceive. Now let's proceed a step further: "Do the things we perceive have an actual existence or are they imaginary?"

Let's start by asking: is there a need for the external world in order to see or hear?

No. There is by no means a need for the external world in order to see or hear. Stimulation of the brain in any form triggers the functioning of all the senses, forming feelings, visions and noises. The best example explaining this reality is the dream.

When we consider this fact deeply, we encounter quite astonishing facts. The brain, where our sensory centres are located, is only a piece of meat weighing 1,400 grams. And this piece of meat is protected in the skull, a mass of bones. This is such a protection that no light, noise, odour of any kind can penetrate through this bony structure. The inside of the skull is pitch-dark and completely insulated from any light and odour. However in this dark space, we live in a colourful world of millions of different tastes, odours and voices. How then does this happen?

What makes you feel the light in pitch-darkness? What makes you feel the odour in a place completely insulated from every kind of odour? Alternatively, what makes you feel other feelings? Who creates all of these senses for you? In fact, every moment a miracle happens...While engrossed with everyday routines, you must never plead ignorance about the extraordinary nature of the situation you experience.

While dreaming, you lie on your bed, in a dark and quiet room, your eyes shut tight. Nothing reaches you from outside for you to perceive... neither light nor noise. However in your dreams, you experience any of the things you are likely to experience in your daily life, just as vividly and clearly as in reality. In your dreams, you also wake up and hurry to work. Alternatively, in your dreams you go on a holiday and feel the summer sunshine.

Besides, during the course of your dreams, you feel no doubts about what you see. Only waking up makes you realise that it was all a dream. In your dreams, you fear, feel anxious, happy or sorry. Simultaneously, you experience the solidity of matter. However, there exists no source producing these perceptions. You are still in a dark and quiet room.

Descartes states the following about this astonishing fact of dreams:

In my dreams, I see that I do various things, I go various places; when I wake up, however, I see that I have not done anything, gone anywhere, and that I peacefully lie in my bed. Who can guarantee to me that I do not dream also at the time being, and even more, that my whole life is not a dream?[17]

In this case, just as we experience our dreams as real and only realise that it was a world of fancy when we awake, we cannot claim that what we experience when awake is real. So, it is entirely probable that, we may well at any time be awoken from the life on earth, which we think we are living right now, and start experiencing real life. We have no evidence with which to deny it. On the contrary, the findings of modern science raise serious doubts about the assertion that what we experience in our daily lives has actual existence.

Someone who hears this for the first time is likely to react in the following way: "I hold with my hand, see with my eyes, so they all exist." Yet one should also think about the following: in dreams, that person also holds with his hand, sees with his eye and even experiences everything as if everything is real. He enjoys, feels fear and pain, takes pleasure…yet, he suddenly wakes up realising that it was only a dream. This is exactly the nature of the life in this world. One day man will wake up from this life as if from a dream and he will face real life.

In this case, we come face to face with an OBVIOUS fact: while we think that this world in which we live exists, there is no ground on which to base this supposition. It is entirely possible that these perceptions do not have material correlates. Since this is so obvious, **you must never plead ignorance that what you see, hear, feel and touch, in brief the "things" you acknowledge as the material world, are only images presented to you.**

If the thing we acknowledge as the material world is merely comprised of perceptions shown to us, then what is the brain, by which we hear, see and think? Isn't the brain, like everything else, a collection of atoms and molecules?

Like everything else we consider "matter", our brains are also perception… it is surely no exception. After all, our brains are also pieces of meat that we perceive by our senses. Like everything we assume to exist in the outer world, it is only an image for us.

So, who perceives all these? Who sees, hears, smells and tastes?

All these bring us face to face with an OBVIOUS fact: a human being who sees, feels, thinks and is conscious is more than just the sum of the atoms and molecules which make up his body. What makes a person a human being is actually the SPIRIT Allah grants him. Otherwise, attribution of consciousness and all human attributes and skills to a piece of meat of 1.5 kg would be definitely irrational, not to mention that this piece of meat is only an illusion. That is why, **you must never plead ignorance that what makes you a person is the spirit Allah "breathed into" you.**

He Who has created all things in the best possible way. He commenced the creation of man from clay; then produced his seed from an extract of base fluid; then formed him and breathed His Spirit into him and gave you hearing, sight and hearts. What little thanks you show! (Surat as-Sajdah: 7-9)

Since a person is not a heap of matter but a "spirit", who presents, or to put it more accurately "creates" and presents, the collection of perceptions called "matter" to our spirits?

The answer to this question is explicit: Allah, Who "breathes" His spirit into human beings, is the creator of everything surrounding us. The only source of these perceptions is Allah. Nothing exists but what He creates. In the following verse, Allah relates that He perpetually creates everything and that otherwise, nothing will continue to exist:

> **Allah keeps a firm hold on the heavens and the earth, preventing them from vanishing away. And if they vanished no one could then keep hold of them. Certainly He is Most Forbearing, Ever-Forgiving. (Surah Fatir: 41)**

Another astonishing fact is that, apart from colours, odours, tastes and voices, "width" and "distance" are also perceived in the brain.

As mentioned above, all perceptions of the room we are in, for instance, are transformed into electrical signals and transmitted to our brains. The sensations transmitted to the brain are interpreted as the image of the room. In other words, you are, in truth, not inside the room you assume you are in; on the contrary, the room is inside you. The location of the room remains in the brain, or rather let us say, the location in which it is perceived in the brain is a tiny, dark and quiet spot. However, the vast landscapes you see on the horizon somehow also fit into this tiny spot. You perceive both the room you are in and the vast landscape in the same place.

Maybe this is something you have never thought about until today. Yet, now you have been reminded of it. So, never plead ignorance that, just like concepts such as distance and width, vast landscapes and narrow rooms are also inside you.

In truth, every individual is enclosed within his own image that is presented to him by his senses. Everyone has his own world. In this world, it is unlikely for anyone to know what others experience or see. Furthermore, one can never know if others see anything or not. That is because, like every other thing, people too are images perceived within his world (brain). This is actually the most important secret of your life.

As a result of the steady conditioning people are exposed to from the time they are born, they may be unwilling to accept this fact. Yet, no matter how they avoid hearing or seeing it, this is an OBVIOUS fact. All the images shown man remain only creations of Allah. Moreover, not only the external world but also all the actions one claims as one's own happen only by the will of Allah. Any action independent and separate from the will of Allah is out of question.

... Allah created both you and what you do. (Surat as-Saffat:96)

... you did not throw when you threw; it was Allah who threw (Surat al-Anfal: 17)

As a result of all these we understand that the only absolute being is Allah. There is nothing but Him. He encompasses everything in the heavens, earth and everything in between. Allah relates in the Qur'an that He is everywhere and that He encompasses all things:

What! Are they in doubt about the meeting with their Lord? What! Does He not encompass all things! (Surah Fussilat: 54)

Both East and West belong to Allah, so whereever you turn, the Face of Allah is there. Allah is All-Encompassing, All-Knowing. (Surat al-Baqarah: 115)

What is in the heavens and in the earth belongs to Allah. Allah encompasses all things.(Surat an-Nisa: 126)

When We said to you, "Surely your Lord encompasses the people with His knowledge." (Surat al-Isra: 60)

Allah, there is no god but Him, the Living, the Self-Sustaining. He is not subject to drowsiness or sleep. Everything in the heavens and the earth belongs to Him. Who can intercede with Him except by His permission? He knows what is before them and what is behind them but they cannot grasp any of His knowledge save what He wills. His Footstool encompasses the heavens and the earth and their preservation does not tire Him. He is the Most High, the Magnificient. (Surat al-Baqarah: 255)

You must never plead ignorance of the fact that Allah encompasses you and He is with you every moment in at every place and that He witnesses everything you do and He is nearer to man than his jugular vein.

Never Plead Ignorance

that Time is a Variable Perception and that Everything is Predestined

*T*ime is also a kind of perception resulting from conclusions we make from our sensory experience. This perception occurs as a result of apparently consecutive events taking place. We perceive the flow of time by comparing the changes in motions we observe one with another. We hear the door ringing, for instance. Ten minutes later it rings again. We perceive that there is an interval between the first ring and second, and interpret this interval as "time". Alternatively, a glass falls and breaks, coal burns and becomes ashes, we walk and find ourselves in one corner of the room while a moment ago we were in the opposite corner. The time passing between these causes and effects and the movements we observe around us gives us clues about the passage of time. Our past experiences also provide us clues enabling us to make almost accurate estimates about how much time an event needs to takes place. If we measure that it takes 10 minutes to walk from home to the nearest bus station, we can assume that it will take approximately 10 minutes to walk the same distance again. Yet someone who is asked how long it takes to walk this distance will probably have little idea if he has never walked that distance before, except according to his experience of having walked similar distances.

The sun rises, sets and by the time it again rises the next day, we say, "a day passed by." When this process is repeated for 30 or 31 days, we say this time, "A month passed." Yet, if you were asked about that month, you would confess that the whole month passed like a moment, realising that you do not recall many details about that month. Still, all the cause and effect relations together with all the actions we observe give us clues about time. If night did not follow day and we did not have a watch indicating the time, we would probably arrive at erroneous conclusions about how many minutes or hours passed by or when the day begins and ends. That is why time is, in fact, a perception we can never comprehend without the existence of points of comparison.

The way time's flow is perceived also shows that time is only a psychological perception. While you are waiting for your friend in the middle of a street, a ten minutes' delay seems like a long, almost everlasting period of time. Alternatively, a person who hasn't had enough sleep at night may perceive a ten minutes' nap in the morning as very long and relaxing. Sometimes just the contrary happens. At school, a boring forty minutes' lesson may seem to be like ages while a ten minutes break passes very quickly. Or, you perceive the weekend you impatiently await as a very short period of time while working days seem long.

No doubt, these are the feelings, shared by almost everyone, indicating that time changes according to the one who perceives it and his state. **You must never plead ignorance about this OBVIOUS fact, which you also experience.**

Allah, in the Qur'an, draws our attention to the fact that time is a psychological perception:

> **He will say: "How many years did you tarry on the earth?" They will say: "We tarried there for a day or part of a day. Ask those who keep account." (Surat al-Muminun: 112-113)**
>
> **On the Day He calls you, you will respond by praising Him and think that you have only tarried a very short time. (Surat al-Isra: 52)**
>
> **On the day We gather them together – when it will seem if they had tarried no more than an hour of a single day – they will recognise one another. Those who denied the meeting with Allah will have lost. They were not guided. (Surah Yunus: 45)**

As the verses above also indicate, the perception of time changes from one person to another. What remains from a life which seemed to be everlasting, yet which ends abruptly, are only reminiscences that would occupy five to ten sheets of paper. In other verses, Allah relates that time takes different forms according to different conditions. Allah says:

The angels and the spirit ascend to Him in a day whose length is fifty thousand years. (Surat al-Ma'arij: 4)

He directs the whole affair from heaven to earth. Then it will again ascend to Him on a day whose length is a thousand years by the way you measure. (Surat as-Sajdah: 5)

Allah creates our perception of time. Allah, the Creator of time, is by no means dependent on it. This is a crucial fact and it provides the answer to a crucial question asked by many people: what is destiny?

The majority of people experience difficulty in understanding the meaning of the concept of destiny.

Destiny is the eternal knowledge of Allah, Who is independent of time and Who prevails over the whole of time and space, about all occurrences and situations of all the beings that are dependent on time. Allah is the Creator of all these actions and situations just as He is the Creator of "time." In the same way as we easily see a ruler's beginning, middle, and end, and all the units in between as a whole, Allah knows the time to which we are subject to as if it were a single moment right from its beginning to its end.

No doubt, this is certain. Allah, Who is not bound by the relative time-frame within which we are confined, encompasses everything time-related. **So, never plead ignorance that All-Mighty Allah created you and that every important or insignificant occurrence you encounter in life is within the knowledge of Allah and predestined.**

Despite this OBVIOUS fact, the majority of people have a distorted understanding of destiny. They assume that they can step out of the boundaries of destiny, "overcome their destiny" or they can live a life separate and independent from destiny. However, as stated earlier, our destinies are in the eternal knowledge of Allah and Allah knows all incidents in the past, present and future, as a single moment. It is unlikely that human beings, who are subject to time, can exceed the boundaries of this single moment and change anything or manage it by their own will. To claim the contrary would be irrational.

We are again face to face with an irrefutable fact: it is implausible that one can change or divert one's own destiny. Surely, the existence of every moment of one's life is dependent upon the exercise of the will of Allah and man cannot do anything, even he cannot think, without the will of Allah. **So, never plead ignorance of this CERTAIN fact.**

Conclusion

*I*n this book, we drew your attention to some facts, which are often left unthought due to mundane realities and everyday problems. These are the most crucial facts for a man in this life. Now, let's review what these facts are:

The existence of Allah, the Creator of everything,

That no process called evolution occurred on earth, that everything is concrete evidence of the glorious creation of Allah,

That man cannot ignore even the miraculous fly, beating its wings 500 times a second,

That various foods and other beauties are all favours of Allah,

That 3-5 decades pass in what can seem like 3-5 seconds,

That after this fleeting life every soul will face the fact of death,

That every soul will be resurrected after death and stand before its Creator for judgement,

That after this judgement each soul will either end up in Paradise or Hell,

That adherence to the Qur'an, the only guidance to the path of Allah, is essential to attain Paradise and certainly one has to conduct oneself as commanded by Allah.

No doubt, one has to ponder deeply each one of these facts. A man who is unaware of these facts or who does not pay due consideration surely risks suffering a great loss, and deep regret. Someone, however, taking such a risk, should consider the following:

The facts discussed in the last chapters of this work render all ambitions and profound attachment to this life meaningless. That is simply because, he is face to face with an EXTRAORDINARY reality; that the world in which he lives, all assets he possesses and people he loves or hates, have no material correlates, because each one of them are illusions constantly created by Allah.

Under these circumstances, is it reasonable for man to be deceived by these illusions and waste his life, which Allah granted him as an opportunity to attain Paradise, in the cause of vain pursuits?

The answer is surely "No."

Someone who is aware of the existence of Allah and hence praises his Creator, never conducts himself in such an unwise manner. Only disbelievers have the imprudence to conduct themselves in such a manner. Allah relates the end of those who spend their whole lives chasing vain pursuits and who forget their Creator:

> **But the actions of those who are unbelievers are like a mirage in the desert. A thirsty man thinks it is water but when he reaches it, he finds it to be nothing at all, but he finds Allah there. He will pay him his account in full. Allah is swift at reckoning. (Surat an-Nur: 39)**

Don't be deceived by assuming that this world, which is only an "illusion" shown to you by Allah, has any absolute existence. Hasten to attain Paradise, where Allah will present all His favours bountifully for all eternity and you should Never Plead Ignorance because then you will face eternal loss.

They said 'Glory be to You! We have no knowledge except what You have taught us. You are the All-Knowing, the All-Wise.' (Surat al-Baqarah: 32)

SOURCES:

1. Robert Shapiro, *Origins: A Sceptics Guide to the Creation of Life on Earth,* New York: Summit Books, 1086, p. 127

2. Fred Hoyle, Chandra Wickramasinghe, *Evolution from Space,* New York: Simon and Schuster, 1984, p. 148

3. Boyse Rensberger, *The Washington Post,* 19 November 1984

4. *The Marvels of Animal Behaviour,* National Geographic Society, 1972, p. 59

5. New Scientist, Eugene Potapov, *How Salemenders Survive the Deep Freeze,* Vol. 139, 11 September 1993, p. 15

6. *Bilim ve Teknik (Science and Technics) Magazine,* October 1987, No. 239, p. 10

7. *Bilim ve Teknik (Science and Technics) Magazine,* Vol. 20, No. 231, February 1987, p. 11

8. Lawrance O.Richards, *It Couldn't Just Happen,* p. 108

9. *Gorsel Bilim ve Teknik Ansiklopedisi (Gorsel Encyclopaedia of Science and Technics),* Vol. 3, p.782

10. *Gorsel Bilim ve Teknik Ansiklopedisi (Gorsel Encyclopaedia of Science and Technics),* Vol. 3, p.784

11. *Gorsel Bilim ve Teknik Ansiklopedisi (Gorsel Encyclopaedia of Science and Technics),* Vol. 7, p.2352

12. *National Geography,* June 1995, No. 6, Vol. 187, p. 50

13. *Gorsel Bilim ve Teknik Ansiklopedisi* (Gorsel Encyclopaedia of Science and Technics), Vol. 8, p.2660

14. David Attenborough, *The Life of Birds,* Princeton, New Jersey: Princeton University Press, 1998, p. 59

15. Pierre P. Grasse, *Evolution of Living Organisms,* New York: Academic Press 1977, p. 103

16. Taskin Tuna, *Uzayin Otesi (Beyond Space),* p. 194

17. Macit Gokberk, *Felsefe Tarihi (History of Philosophy),* p.263

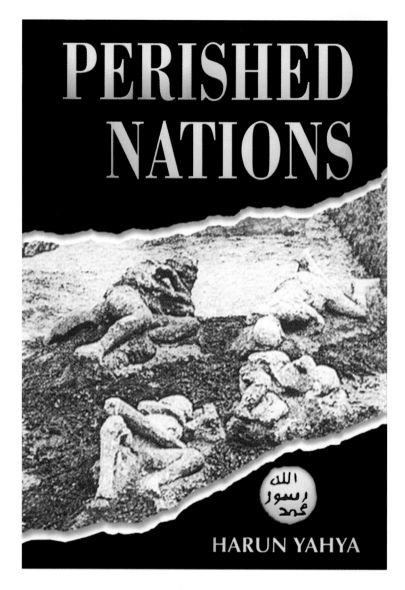

PERISHED NATIONS

HARUN YAHYA

Many societies that rebelled against the will of Allah or regarded His messengers as enemies were wiped off the face of the earth completely... All of them were destroyed–some by a volcanic eruption, some by a disastrous flood, and some by a sand storm...

Perished Nations examines these penalties as revealed in the verses of the Quran and in light of archaeological discoveries.

149 PAGES WITH 73 PICTURES
IN COLOUR

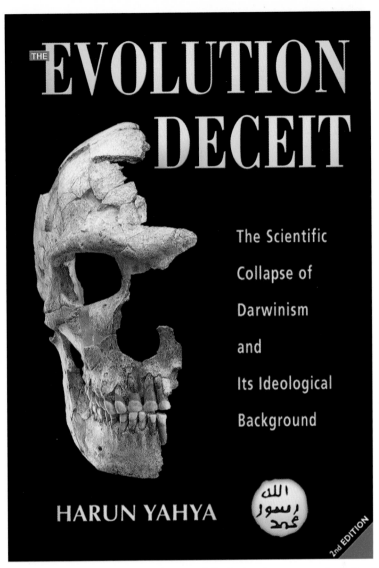

THE EVOLUTION DECEIT

The Scientific Collapse of Darwinism and Its Ideological Background

HARUN YAHYA

2nd EDITION

Many people think that Darwin's Theory of Evolution is a proven fact. Contrary to this conventional wisdom, recent developments in science completely disprove the theory. The only reason Darwinism is still foisted on people by means of a worldwide propaganda campaign lies in the ideological aspects of the theory. All secular ideologies and philosophies try to provide a basis for themselves by relying on the theory of evolution.

This book clarifies the scientific collapse of the theory of evolution in a way that is detailed but easy to understand. It reveals the frauds and distortions committed by evolutionists to "prove" evolution. Finally it analyzes the powers and motives that strive to keep this theory alive and make people believe in it.

Anyone who wants to learn about the origin of living things, including mankind, needs to read this book.

238 PAGES WITH 166 PICTURES
IN COLOUR

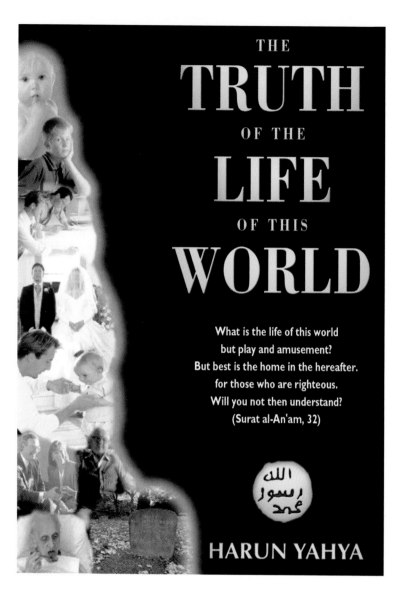

THE TRUTH OF THE LIFE OF THIS WORLD

What is the life of this world
but play and amusement?
But best is the home in the hereafter.
for those who are righteous.
Will you not then understand?
(Surat al-An'am, 32)

HARUN YAHYA

One of the major reasons why people feel a profound sense of attachment to life and cast religion aside is the assumption that life is eternal. Forgetting that death is likely to put an end to this life at any time, man simply believes that he can enjoy a perfect and happy life. Yet he evidently deceives himself. The world is a temporary place specially created by Allah to test man. That is why, it is inherently flawed and far from satisfying man's endless needs and desires. Each and every attraction existing in the world eventually wears out, becomes corrupt, decays and finally disappears. This is the never-changing reality of life.

This book explains this most important essence of life and leads man to ponder the real place to which he belongs, namely the Hereafter.

224 PAGES WITH 144 PICTURES IN COLOUR

SIGNS IN THE HEAVENS AND THE EARTH

FOR MEN
OF
UNDERSTANDING

HARUN YAHYA

One of the purposes why the Qur'an was revealed is to summon people to think about creation and its works. When a person examines his own body or any other living thing in nature, the world or the whole universe, in it he sees a great design, art, plan and intelligence. All this is evidence proving Allah's being, unit, and eternal power.

For Men of Understanding was written to make the reader see and realise some of the evidence of creation in nature. Many living miracles are revealed in the book with hundreds of pictures and brief explanations.

288 PAGES WITH 467 PICTURES IN COLOUR

DEEP THINKING

In the creationof the heavens and the earth, and the alternation of night and day, there are signs for people with intelligence: those who remember Allah, standing, sitting and lying on their sides, and reflect on the creation of the heavens and the earth: 'Our Lord, You have not created this for nothing. Glory be to You! So safeguard us from the punishment of the Fire!' (Surat Al 'Imran: 191)

HARUN YAHYA

Have you ever thought that you were non-existent before you were born and suddenly appeared on Earth? Have you ever thought that the peel of a banana, melon, watermelon or an orange each serve as a quality package preserving the fruit's odour and taste?

Man is a being to which Allah has granted the faculty of thinking. Yet a majority of people fail to employ this faculty as they should… The purpose of this book is to summon people to think in the way they should and to guide them in their efforts to think.

128 PAGES WITH 137 PICTURES IN COLOUR

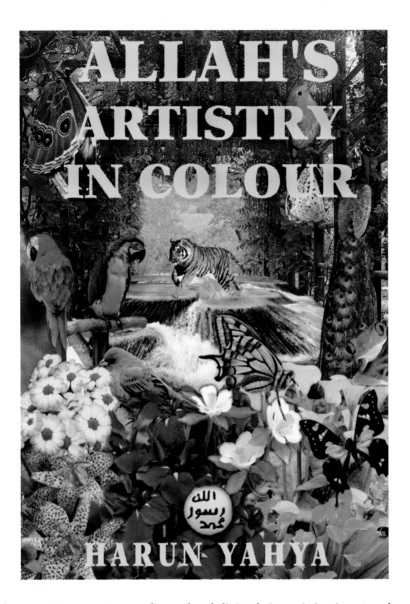

ALLAH'S ARTISTRY IN COLOUR

HARUN YAHYA

Colours, patterns, spots, even lines of each living being existing in nature have a meaning. For some species, colours serve as a communication tool; for others, they are a warning against enemies. Whatever the case, these colours are essential for the well-being of living beings. An attentive eye would immediately recognise that not only the living beings, but also everything in nature are just as they should be. Furthermore, he would realise that everything is given to the service of man: the comforting blue colour of the sky, the colourful view of flowers, the bright green trees and meadows, the moon and stars illuminating the world in pitch darkness together with innumerable beauties surrounding man…

160 PAGES WITH 215 PICTURES IN COLOUR

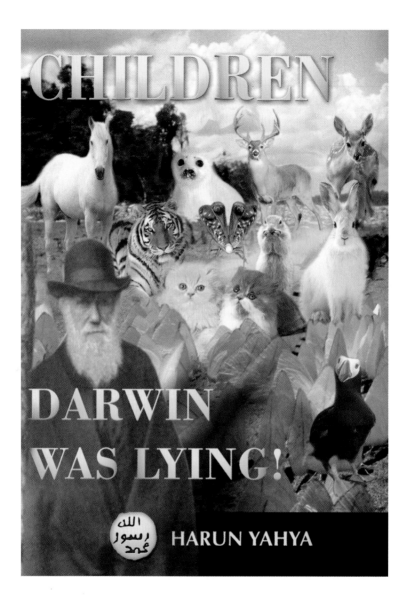

CHILDREN

DARWIN WAS LYING!

HARUN YAHYA

Children!

Have you ever asked yourself questions like these: How did our earth come into existence? How did the moon and sun come into being? Where were you before you were born? How did oceans, trees, animals appear on earth? How do your favourite fruits –bananas, cherries, plums– with all their bright colours and pleasant scents grow in black soil? How does a little tiny bee know how to produce delicious honey? How can it build a honeycomb with such astonishingly regular edges? Who was the first human being? Your mom gave birth to you. Yet the first human being could not have had parents. So, how did he come into existence?" In this book you will find the true answers to these questions.

144 PAGES WITH 282 PICTURES
IN COLOUR

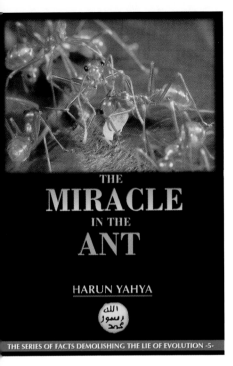

THE
MIRACLE
IN THE
ANT

HARUN YAHYA

THE SERIES OF FACTS DEMOLISHING THE LIE OF EVOLUTION -5-

The evidence of Allah's creation is present everywhere in the universe. A person comes across many of these proofs in the course of his daily life; yet if he does not think deeply, he may wrongly consider them to be trivial details. In fact in every creature there are great mysteries to be pondered.

These millimeter-sized animals that we frequently come across but don't care much about have an excellent ability for organization and specialization that is not to be matched by any other being on earth. These aspects of ants create in one a great admiration for Allah's superior power and unmatched creation.

165 PAGES WITH 104 PICTURES IN COLOUR

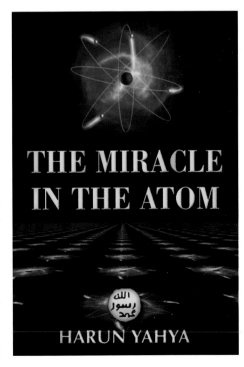

THE MIRACLE
IN THE ATOM

HARUN YAHYA

In a body that is made up of atoms, you breathe in air, eat food, and drink liquids that are all composed of atoms. Everything you see is nothing but the result of the collision of electrons of atoms with photons.

In this book, the implausibility of the spontaneous formation of an atom, the building-block of everything, living or non-living, is related and the flawless nature of Allah's creation is demonstrated.

139 PAGES WITH 122 PICTURES IN COLOUR

**SOLUTION
THE MORALS OF
THE QUR'AN**

Mischief has appeared on land and sea because of
(the meed) that the hands of men have earned,
that (Allah) may give them a taste of some of their
deeds; in order that they may turn back (from Evil).
(Surat Al-Rum: 41)

HARUN YAHYA

People who are oppressed, who are tortured to death, innocent babies, those who cannot afford even a loaf of bread, who must sleep in tents or even in streets in cold weather, those who are massacred just because they belong to a certain tribe, women, children, and old people who are expelled from their homes because of their religion... Eventually, there is only one solution to the injustice, chaos, terror, massacres, hunger, poverty, and oppression: the morals of the Qur'an.

208 PAGES WITH 276 PICTURES IN COLOUR

**JESUS
WILL COME**

"When the angels said, "Maryam, your Lord gives
you good news of a Word from Him.
His name is the Messiah, Isa, son of
Maryam of high esteem in
the world and the hereafter"
(Surat Ali Imran:45)

HARUN YAHYA

In the Qur'an, there is an explicit reference to the "second coming of the Jesus to the world" which is heralded in a hadith. The realisation of some information revealed in the Qur'an about Jesus can only be possible by Jesus' second coming...

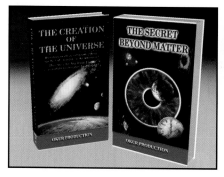

VHS VIDEO CASSETTES